GOOD SPORTS

The Concerned Parent's Guide to
Competitive Youth Sports

by
Rick Wolff

ISBN: 1-57167-048-3
Library of Congress Catalog Card Number: 96-71927

Book layout: Antonio J. Perez
Cover design: Deborah M. Bellaire
Proofreader: Laura J. Canham-Perez
Author and back cover photos: Rick Wolff photo courtesy of Vin Holland
Front cover photos: Coaching and gymnast photos courtesy of McKinley Family YMCA, Champaign, IL.
Soccer photo by John Seder, Champaign Park District, Champaign, IL.
Baseball photo by Marilyn Cundiff

Sports Publishing Inc.
804 N. Neil
Champaign, IL 61820

www.sportspublishinginc.com

For John, Alyssa, and Samantha

—the best coaches I've ever had

ACKNOWLEDGMENTS

Putting together a book is no small task, and I'm gratefully indebted to the following people for their kind assistance and encouragement along the way: Dr. Rainer Martens, of Human Kinetics; psychologists Dr. Jim Richard and Ruthmary Richard, M.A.; the creative writing team of Bruce Nash and Allan Zullo; Neil Judge, director of athletics at Mercy College; the entire Cleveland Indians baseball organization; sportscaster Bob Wolff; Hall of Famer Rod Carew; Tom Grieve, general manager of the Texas Rangers; attorney Mel Narol, Esq.; columnist Phil Mushnick; author Jim Charlton; and Jeanine Bucek of Sports Illustrated for Kids books.

I'd also like to specially to thank my editors, Leslie Schnur, Jill Lamar, and Peter Bannon for their enthusiasm and patience during this project. Believe me, I know how difficult it can be to edit a sports book.

And finally, my thanks to Trish. Quite simply, she's the best.

PREFACE

Does an entire book have to be written about how to let kids have fun and enjoy themselves when they play sports?

Is it that difficult these days to know how to coach, motivate, and work with children? Sure, times have changed a bit since we were growing up, but let's face facts—aren't kids still, for the most part, just kids?

All good, legitimate questions. The kinds of questions I would have asked before I had children of my own. After all, we've all heard the horror stories involving organized youth sports leagues: the fights between coaches, the overbearing parents, the eruption of on-the-field arguments, kids rejecting sports for a variety of reasons. The average onlooker hears and reads about these incidents and just assumes that these incredible, outlandish acts of crazed coaches and parents are nothing more than aberrations or a statistical flukes.

But those of us who are immersed in organized youth sports know better. We know that while loud, disruptive episodes tend to be nothing more than the tip of the youth league iceberg, we also recognize that there are a lot of uneasy signals coming out of our kids' sports leagues in the 1990s. These worrisome signals are early warning signs that the leagues in which our kids play are either flat out of sync with our educational priorities or just not emphasizing fun enough. Either way, if you care about your kids' development in sports, it's time to get involved.

Out of these realities, the urge to write this book was born. A product of organized youth leagues myself, and having gone on to a highly enjoyable career as a professional athlete, college coach, and sports psychology consultant, I know firsthand that it's not easy to keep one's priorities fully in order when the competition heats up out on the playing field.

But that's precisely when the adult in us should take over, reminding us that we are dealing with kids here— and what we're doing with organized youth leagues is for the kids' benefit, not our own.

As you go through this book, you will see lots of situations readily recognizable from your own experience. Ideally, some of the thoughts and suggestions here will help you and your family cope with the realities of competitive sports for young people. At the very least they will get you thinking about sports in your community, and whether or not those sports leagues are doing the best they can for your children.

In sum, my purpose in writing this book was to accomplish one simple goal: to allow children of all ages to fully embrace and enjoy the wonder, challenge, and fun of playing sports. Teaching, coaching, motivating, and winning at sports are all fine for kids—but most important of all, I want my kids to have fun. And I imagine you want the same for your kids too.

CONTENTS

CHAPTER 1

Goal Setting—
What Do You Want for Your Child?

This book is written for those parents who have children who like sports—any sports—and who are eager to participate in organized youth teams within their community. Defining our terms, an "organized youth team" is a part of any league within your town that has a structure that has been set up and is run by parents like yourself. The common parameters of these leagues, which include such well-known organizations as Little League baseball, AYSO soccer, Pony League baseball, Pee-Wee football and U.S.A. ice hockey, and others, usually involve volunteer parent coaches, team uniforms, schedules, referees/umpires, and, in many cases, an ongoing compilation of team win/loss records.

These leagues usually start with kids as young as age five, and for the purposes of this book I've aimed my comments at boys and girls up to the age of twelve or thirteen. At fourteen or older they are entering high school and participate primarily on high school teams coached by professional educators, not volunteer mothers and fathers.

It is important to make a most vital point regarding these organized youth leagues, and that is, in most cases these leagues tend to be positive, enriching experiences for the children and their parents. That's the good news.

The bad news is that for many children, these early years in organized youth sports can result in a lot of bad experiences as well. There are just too many cases of kids who, first introduced to sports in a highly competitive environment, a few years later have decided to shut sports out of their lives. Instead of going on to enjoy amateur sports at the high school level, these youngsters have instead turned away from sports. And that, of course, is a tragedy that could have been avoided.

Some Basic Ground Rules

The purpose of this chapter is to set forth some of the basic themes that will run throughout this book, and that will serve as your guidelines as you shepherd your child through organized youth sports. But without a doubt the most important question you have to ask yourself through this experience is the following:

> *When you sign your son or daughter up with a youth sports team, what is your goal for your child?*

The answer to that one question may seem simple or obvious, but it's not. Too many parents go through the process of signing their kids up for organized youth sports without giving it a second thought; it's as though youth sports are merely a rite of passage in every American town, simply a part of growing up that has become totally reflexive in our society.

But if you take the time to think about organized youth sports and what you want your child to experience from them, you'll find you've taken the first step to making your child's athletic experience a positive one. For example, do you want your child to use youth sports as a pathway to a professional sports career? Or do you simply want your child to enjoy him- or herself? Do you want her to learn about team play and sportsmanship? Or do you merely want your child to get some exercise and fresh air?

There are more questions to ponder. Do you have total trust and faith in the people who are coaching your child? What will you do if your child comes home and hasn't enjoyed the experience? What do you do if your child cares only about winning and nothing else? What do you do if your child doesn't play by the rules, or doesn't even understand them? What if your child comes home upset because the coach has yelled at him or her during practice? And what do you do if your child isn't as good as his or her peers—do you yank him off the team or tell him to be patient, that he'll develop his skills as the season goes along?

Too many questions? Perhaps. But it has always struck me as somewhat curious that concerned parents will spend so much time worrying about finding the proper school system or teacher for their children, and then seemingly become totally apathetic regarding their child's participation on a youth sports team.

You know what I'm talking about: some parents watch their child's progress in school on a daily basis. If there's even the slightest suggestion that the teacher isn't totally motivating their child, Mom and Dad can't wait to call the school principal or write a nasty note to the school board. But talk to those same parents about youth sports in their town and it becomes a totally different story. It's almost as though soccer, baseball, or basketball practice is just another weekend baby-sitting session in which the parent can drop the kid off and not be worried about him or her for an hour or so. So let's clear up some basic misunderstandings before we even get underway.

The Odds are Already Stacked Against You

For many proud moms and dads one of the most gratifying experiences in life is to daydream that your son is destined to grow up to be the next Mickey Mantle or that your daughter will someday become the next Katarina Witt. While certainly no one is suggesting that you should ever stop pursuing your dreams, please keep in mind that as an adult and parent you must maintain a solid grasp on reality.

Specifically, it's been well documented that the odds of a top high school player making the professional ranks in any sport are literally hundreds of thousands to one. And that's for proven high school stars. I'm talking about the cream of the high school crop, the kids who make All-State, All-City, or All-County teams; when you see your son as the next Michael Jordan or daughter as the next Chris Evert, bear in mind that you probably have as good a chance of winning the state lottery as seeing your kid becoming a millionaire professional athlete.

When you start focusing on kids between the ages of six and thirteen to become professional athletes, the odds become even more enormous. This is not meant to discourage a youngster from having dreams; rather, it's for you, the parent, to accept a dosage of adult reality.

Playing the Numbers Game

A few years ago a study was done on young athletes to see how many top players from the youth leagues ever went on to become top players in high school. In other words, the study was designed to see if the stars of the organized youth leagues would become the stars of high school.

The results indicated that only 25 percent, or one out of every four youth league stars, ever end up becoming stars just a few years later in high school.[1] Why? A number of factors come into play, including how the youngster physically matures, how her interests develop, how dedicated and disciplined she is to practicing her skills, and what kind of coaching she receives. But the point is well taken; only one out of every four stars in youth sports is destined to become a star in high school. The odds are even greater against your child someday signing a pro contract.

When working with college and professional athletes I often remind them that in the world of highly competitive sports there's a natural pyramid of success that every athlete (and parent) has to deal with. On the bottom of that pyramid are all the wonderfully talented kids who play youth sports. But as you begin to climb that pyramid you find that only a certain percentage of those athletically gifted kids ever go on to become high school players. Then, going farther up the pyramid, the competition becomes even stiffer: only a small percentage of high school athletes are ever good enough to make a college team. And, of course, at the top of the pyramid are those few who make the professional ranks. It's quite a narrowing process.

But the aim of this book is not to make your six year old into a professional athlete. Rather, it's to get your kids to enjoy sports, to enjoy the inherent thrill of being on a youth team and of seeing their athletic skills improve as they mature.

Rule #1: Don't Sit Back! Get Involved

Now that we have all of the bad news out of the way, let's make some positive statements. First of all, if you're going to put your child in a youth league have enough interest and responsibility to get involved yourself and stay involved.

Sports—even at the earliest ages—are competitive in nature. Competition does not have to be a negative aspect of youth sports. Indeed, the world revolves around competition, and simply trying to shun it or ignore it will not do you or your child any good. Competition should be positive.

Are there opposing views to competition? Of course. In *No Contest: The Case Against Competition*, author Alfie Kohn insists that competition, especially in sports, is to be avoided at all costs.[2] While I agree with Kohn that too much competition can destroy much of a child's innate pleasure in playing sports and games, I also feel that such competitive drives can be kept in perspective if the kids' parents are attentive and stay involved, preventing things from getting out of hand.

Yet the fact remains that too much competition can quickly sour a positive experience in sports if you aren't careful. In today's world you want your child to learn and comprehend from competition, not shy away from it. You want to prepare him for competition the same way you want to prepare him to read and write and do arithmetic.

Competition at the youngest levels of sport should always be kept in its purest and simplest form. Keeping score is not necessary in the youngest leagues (five to seven years old), and talk of winning and losing should be minimized. When your six or seven year old comes off the field and asks, "Did we win?" it's absolutely vital for you to say, "All I care about is that you had a good time. You certainly played very well."

As the child gets older, competition and concerns about winning and losing will become more a part of his/her life. But keeping it all in perspective is absolutely essential. You, as the adult, have to provide that balance for your child.

As a parent it's your obligation to get involved with your child's sports team. You know the typical experience: there's a flyer that goes around the community that a certain youth sport league is having a sign-up session on a particular Saturday. Sure enough, all the kids in elementary school sign up for the league, but when it says on the sign-up sheet that parents are "eagerly invited to help out" with coaching, it's almost impossible to get any grown-up to help out. Do any of these excuses sound familiar?

- "I'm sorry, but I have to work on the weekends."

- "Oh, I don't know anything about baseball (soccer, gymnastics, hockey, etc.)."

- "I wasn't very good at sports myself. What good would I be as a coach?"

- "I'll bring the drinks on game day."

The simple fact of the matter is that you should always get involved, that you should try to coach (even if you know nothing about the sport), and that you should observe what kind of experience your child is having. If you really know very little about the sport, go to the library, get some books on the subject. When you read to your child, you can learn about the sport at the same time.

Remember at all times that seeing how she does against her peers on the athletic field is psychologically very important for your child. To her, sports is not "just another game" but rather an emotional experience for her in her young life.

Even worse, if you don't get involved and your son or daughter ends up playing for an insensitive coach who turns the experience of youth sports into a negative one for your child, then don't put all the blame on the coach. Blame yourself, because it's your fault for being timid and not getting involved.

Rule #2: Keep Track of Your Own Behavior

Now, this is where you may have to work a little because when things get a bit difficult for your child it's up to you to be a constant source of inspiration and optimism. This is not to say that you don't share in your child's pain if he doesn't play well or his team loses a close game. But remember that you are a major role model for your child. The way you behave will go a long way in helping him decide how he should behave.

For most parents this is not an easy task. If you tend to scream, yell, and stomp when things don't go well in your own life—and you show similar tantrums on the athletic field—don't be surprised if your son or daughter imitates those very same behavior patterns.

Quite frankly, there is no place in youth sports for adults to act like spoiled brats. But sad to say, chances are that all of us have seen other parents act this way during a youth sport game. It's not a pretty sight, and honestly, it destroys every positive aspect of youth sports as far as the children are concerned.

A couple of years ago one of these incidents occurred at a soccer game in the town where I live. One of the fathers was irate over a call that a referee had made (mind you, this was a league for six and seven year olds), and he was screaming obscenities at the top of his lungs in a face-to-face confrontation with the ref.

As it developed, one of the parents happened to have a video camera at the game and she taped the ugly incident. When it was played back later to the father who had been so vociferous it was curious to watch his reaction.

At first he tried to laugh the incident off, commenting that he was "just like Billy Martin or Lou Pinella" in his verbal fireworks. But as the tape played on he quickly ended his attempt at humor and the ugliness of the scene began to sink in. He wouldn't stop yelling. He was so wrapped up in making his point heard, he lost sight of the children around him.

As the tape continued to roll he eventually calmed down, but by this time, as an observer, he was able to see that the soccer game between the little kids had stopped and that the children from both teams were watching and listening to him. It may have been the most embarrassing experience of his life. I could only imagine what the kids on the field thought of this ridiculous outburst.

But the sad reality is that this kind of behavior happens in thousands of well-meaning communities all over the country on any given sports weekend. That doesn't make it acceptable—it's just wrong.

Rule #3: Always Be Positive—But Careful—in Your Feedback

Kids play sports for a variety of reasons, many of which seem to be lost on parents. Indeed, some of us honestly seem to forget that when we were kids ourselves we played sports too—and that our priorities then were those of children and not of our parents.

That's an important distinction, and one that will be discussed more fully later. But the point is well taken: the reasons why our kids play and enjoy sports usually have very little in common with the ways in which adults enjoy sports.

More specifically, "winning" and "losing" are abstract concepts that kids tend to learn on their own and in their own way. Children are not genetically programmed to comprehend what victory or defeat means. But kids do quickly pick up on the realization that winning a soccer or Little League game tends to make Mommy and Daddy happy while losing seems to elicit such comments as, "You have to practice more and play harder if you want to win."

Playing for parental approval is one of the most important influences of organized youth sports. It's an influence with far-reaching ramifications that all parents must understand fully. Chances are that you have always heard that, as a parent, you should lavish tons of praise on your little athlete. Look in any coach's manual on how to work with youngsters and it's guaranteed that one of the first rules of coaching is to make everything positive for the child.

While it's true that you should always strive to make the athletic experience a happy one for your child and his/her friends by praising their efforts, you should also recognize that positive feedback comes in different forms and that you have to be careful about the kinds of feedback you're giving.

Example: The other day I was at a Little League baseball game and one of the coaches piped up with, "I'll give anyone on the team who hits a home run a brand new twenty-dollar bill." Now, he certainly didn't do anything criminal or illegal. He merely wanted to motivate his little players to reach their full potential— and if they did that (by hitting a home run), he would reward the effort with a positive reinforcement, i.e., the twenty-dollar bill.

But such a seemingly innocent gesture sets off some warning signs for all the kids. First and foremost, their motivation for hitting a home run has shifted from the pure fun and enjoyment of the moment, to the winning of a cash award. The twenty-dollar bill has become the motivating force, not the enjoyment of hitting a baseball.

Second, the kids all figure that the way to win the money, along with their coach's admiration, is to slug the ball for a homer. Again, parental approval is a strong motivator; in this case the coach serves as the surrogate parent, and every kid on that team wants to win his approval.

Finally, while a few of the bigger and more talented kids on the team may have the potential to hit a home run, chances are that many more kids on the team just aren't physically developed enough yet to even come close to hitting a ball that far. However, because they still want to please their coach as well as win the cash reward, they try their hardest—only to fail in their efforts.

What's the overall take from the coach's challenge? The kids who try to hit a homer and fail tend to go away without having won the twenty dollars and feeling downright discouraged that they didn't capture the admiration and approval of the coach. Plus, they have now begun to transfer the inherent enjoyment of hitting a ball away from simply mastering that skill to pursuing an extrinsic award, namely, the money.

In other words, a relatively simple offer from a coach that was meant "merely to let the kids have more fun" is in reality a needless incentive that's going to yield, for most of the kids, disappointment and discouragement.

This is why it's vital that you always couch your feedback to young players in positive terms, being careful that it doesn't end up backfiring on you and the children.

Example: When I was the head baseball coach at a local college we were fortunate to have successful teams each year. Yet one season things weren't going that well. We seemed to lose our cool in tight games in the late innings. It got to the point that I was searching desperately for answers and I even asked one of the team's seniors if there was anything I was doing wrong as coach.

"Well, as a matter of fact," he said, "I know the guys on the team start to get nervous during close games, and I think it's because the guys start seeing you get nervous on the bench and in the dugout."

In other words, even though I thought I was conducting my outward appearance during games in an appropriate fashion, I was not. I would get nervous, pace the dugout, become very snappy with the team, and tend to raise my voice harshly whenever the score was tied. My players picked up on this behavior, saw how nervous I was, and quickly figured that if the head coach was nervous, well, then they ought to be too.

Sure enough, they would make errors and play with great trepidation, though in calmer times they would play with solid confidence and enthusiasm. I realized that I was giving off all sorts of nervous energy that my players were picking up on. From then on I consciously changed my style and relaxed in close games. The result? My players also began to relax and played with more confidence on the field.

The point is simple. Remember that your kids are constantly watching, observing, and learning from you. In the same way that they'll pick up on your patterns of speech, they're also learning how to react during athletic competition. If you stomp your feet and curse when things go poorly on the field, they'll do that too. If you scream at the ump or ref, your kids will imitate that as well. If you're a poor sport, they'll follow suit.

Rule #4: Kids Learn Behavior from Their Parents

When coaching one of my children's soccer teams last year, we had a very talented little boy on the squad. He was fortunate to have two very bright, very talented parents. But it always made me a bit uncomfortable that whenever the game began the boy's mom would light up cigarette after nervous cigarette while watching her son perform. Between puffs she would scream at the top of her lungs to encourage her boy and the rest of the kids.

Many other parents are the same way. But ask yourself: what's going through the kid's head when he sees you or hears you on the sidelines screaming, shouting, cursing, or pouting? And what happens if he begins to suspect his on-the-field behavior is not pleasing Mommy and Daddy? Sometimes, rather than try living up to your standards, children will either just give up, tell you that they don't want to play anymore, tell you that they're sick or injured, or that they'd rather play something else.

Rule #5: The Potent Combination of Parental Approval and Positive Feedback

Above everything else, remember that kids respond extraordinarily well to positive feedback. B. F. Skinner taught that all organisms (including kids) will respond to any environmental stimulus that tends to benefit that organism's self-interest. From that simple psychological perspective you can understand just how potent a combination of positive feedback and parental approval can become for any youngster. It's up to you, the parent, to make certain that these two elements are used with the right priorities in mind.

Sure, it's difficult. But go back to the first question posed at the beginning of this chapter: What do you want your children to get out of playing organized youth sports?

If you want them only to care about winning and winning all the time, that's easily programmed. Just tell the kids that, "every time they win a game they'll all get free pizza and sodas!" You don't have to work in a psych lab with rats and pigeons to understand that your kids will quickly comprehend that winning means food and treats, and losing means they go hungry.

On the other hand, if you want your kids to understand that in sports, as in life, the concepts of winning and losing should be confronted, handled, and dealt with in a rational way, perhaps a different kind of reward should be used. Perhaps it would make more sense to reward a youngster's efforts for simply playing hard—win or lose—than hitch his reward to winning only.

Don't misunderstand. Kids are still going to be disappointed when they lose. Even in those young leagues where scores are not officially kept kids still have an amazing knack of keeping score themselves. But the point here is not so much whether the kids win or lose, but how they—and you—cope with losing or winning.

Rule #6: This Is Your Kid's Life—Not Yours!

Sounds so simple, but it's so often overlooked. Sorry to have to say this, but your childhood is over. It may have been great or not so great, but in the chronology of life you have to face up to the stark reality that your childhood is over and that you really don't want to live it again through your kids.

Not only is it potentially dangerous to your children, but it is perhaps the most selfish thing a parent can do.

Certainly you want to share in your child's delight as he or she masters an athletic skill, whether it's the first kick of a soccer ball or riding a two-wheeler. But while you're enjoying the thrill of being a kid through your child's eyes, you also have to keep your title of adult and parent close by. It's up to you to know when you're pressing too hard, boasting too much, or acting like a spoiled kid rather than a mature adult.

You've heard the expression "he's living his life through his child." It's okay to be proud of your son or daughter and what he or she can do on the athletic field—but it's not okay to become overbearing and pompous about your kid's abilities. Chances are that if your kid does happen to be one of the better players the other parents and kids see this as well. You don't have to feel obliged to point it out to them. It's been my experience that a little parental modesty goes a long way in keeping everybody on the team happy.

Also, remember, that kids mature physically at different rates. Today's little six-year-old shrimp might be the towering school bully by the time he's eight. The blubbery little blond girl in the third grade might add six inches to her height over the summer and become muscular and strong.

The point is, don't become overly concerned if your son or daughter, at age six, is a "daisy picker" during games, because one year's time for a child makes a big, big difference. As a parent, whether you're 35 or 36 may not make much of a difference in terms of your physical or athletic skills. But for a six year old, turning seven means an entire year of physical growth, psychological self-confidence, and learning about the world. And the physical and mental growth continues right through her entire childhood, and that very much influences the way she plays sports.

Rule #7: You Have to Work at Having Fun

This rule may seem totally contradictory, but the more you think about it the more you'll realize how true it really is.

Remember that a child's perception of sport or play is totally different from yours. Numerous psychological studies done over the years have proven that for a child the process of play is not play at all; rather it is the arduous task of mastering certain skills, such as kicking a ball, running to first base, or catching a ball. For that child, what we perceive too often as "playing ball" is really hard work.

The child will take delight in his success at mastering an athletic skill, but only because he has come to grips with that task and has gained competence in it. Many times this delight will lead him to repeat that accomplished task because he enjoys the feeling of competence that comes with kicking a ball solidly or catching a thrown ball. And with a feeling of competence comes a sense of self-esteem.

Nevertheless, this entire process, which to most adults appears as nothing more than "child's play," is hardly play at all. It is challenging, dutiful hard work for the child; the fun arises out of a sense of accomplishment.

Just how do kids view sports? In a recent poll conducted by *USA Today* and NBC, published in the sports section of *USA Today*,[3] the following observations were made about kids' sports and having fun:

- 71 percent of the kids surveyed said they wouldn't care if no score were kept in their games.

- 37 percent wished that no parents would watch them play sports.

- 41 percent said that they have awakened in the night worrying about an upcoming game.

- 51 percent of the kids said that they see other kids act like poor sports frequently.

No matter how you interpret these observations it is impossible to escape the conclusion that, for many children, learning to play and enjoy organized youth sports is becoming increasingly difficult. Again, the purpose of this book is not to tear down these organized sports leagues, but rather to keep their priorities in order and to make the experience of youth sports as pleasant and as positive as possible for you and your child.

Just remember this one telling statistic: According to the survey, by age 15 more than 75 percent of the kids who started playing organized sports at age six or seven have already stopped playing.

Says Mike Pfahl, executive director of the National Youth Sports Coaches' Association: "How many times do you hear a professional athlete say he's quitting because it's not fun anymore? Well, why should it be different for a seven-, eight-, or nine-year-old child?"

As you read through the following chapters, try to remember the above guidelines about kids and youth sports. Of course, every boy and girl is different and reacts to sports and competition in various ways. But by and large, if you want your children to enjoy their experiences in sports, and want them to stay physically active in sports for the rest of their lives, now is the time to intervene. It is now, as children, that they are forming attitudes about sports, teams, and physical exercise that will affect them the rest of their lives.

1. R. Martens, *Joy and Sadness in Children's Sports* (Champaign, Ill.: Human Kinetics Publishers, 1978), p. 184.
2. A. Kohn, *No Contest: The Case Against Competition* (Boston: Houghton Mifflin, 1988).
3. *USA Today*, September 9, 1990.

CHAPTER 2

What the Experts Say

According to Dr. Rainer Martens, one of the nation's leading psychologists and experts on youth sports, the worries about children and sports seem to run in cycles. "The first wave of concern started in the early 1950s, and then again, there was great controversy about Little League and the like in the early 1970s. Judging from those precedents, I can understand why it is happening again in the 1990s."

Parents' concerns about youth sports have been with us for some time now. But what's curious is that while many well-meaning moms and dads have expressed all sorts of worries about the impact that organized youth sports have on their sons and daughters, precious little has been written about what the experts—the psychologists, psychiatrists, pediatricians, and educators— have to say about these youth leagues. But over the last decade the experts have started to quietly observe children's behavior in these quasi-structured play environments. They've been conducting psychological experiments to see just how children react to sport, play, winning, and losing.

The Best and the Brightest?

Let's start with the athletes themselves. Most parents totally accept the premise that organized youth sports, such as Little League or Pop Warner football, are the launching pad for future major league players.

But what struck me as ironic when I started to ask current and former major leaguers about their experiences in Little League baseball was that one after the other told me that they would never let their own children play in such organized leagues. Ron Leflore a major league star for many seasons with the Tigers, White Sox, and Expos, who now lives in Florida, was adamant that his son not play Little League ball. "Too many parents just don't know what they're doing when they're coaching, and I've seen too many kids hurt by the experience," says Leflore.

I recall what the late Steve Olin, the outstanding relief pitcher for the Cleveland Indians, once told me. Olin, who was tragically killed in a freak boating accident, delivered his pitches in a "submarine" or sidearm style. His unique delivery propelled him right through high school, college, and into the majors.

But growing up as a youngster in Oregon, Olin found coach after coach in youth baseball leagues telling him, "Steve, you can't throw that way—you'll never get to the big leagues throwing sidearm." As Olin continues: "Thank goodness I was a stubborn kid, because even though every coach told me in every league to change my style and throw in the conventional overhand way, I still believed that this sidearm style was the best—and the most fun—for me. In fact, if I had listened to my coaches and changed my delivery to be more conventional I would never have made it at all."

Robin Roberts, a star pitcher for many seasons for the Philadelphia Phillies, is another who has stepped forward about the hazards of youth sports, and in particular about Little League baseball. Writing in an article for *Newsweek*,[1] Roberts says:

> *I still don't know what those ... gentlemen in Williamsport had in mind when they organized Little League baseball. I'm sure they didn't want parents arguing with their children about kids' games. I'm sure they didn't want to have family meals disrupted for three months every year. I'm sure they didn't want young athletes hurting their arms pitching under pressure at such a young age. I'm sure they didn't want young boys who don't have much athletic ability made to feel that something is wrong with them because they can't play baseball. I'm sure they didn't want a group of coaches drafting the players each year for different teams. I'm sure they didn't want unqualified men working with younger players. I'm sure they didn't realize how normal it is for an eight-year-old boy to be scared of a thrown or batted baseball. For the life of me I can't figure out what they had in mind.*

In all fairness to the gentleman who did start Little League baseball it should be pointed out that he is not to blame for the over-commercialization of the sport. Carl Stotz founded Little League in 1939 in his home town of Williamsport, Pennsylvania. Stotz saw the game as nothing more than a grass-roots effort to bring kids into baseball with their parents support.

What Stotz didn't foresee was the incredible popularity of his Little League concept and how quickly it would spread to all parts of the country and then to the world. One of the most important factors in the growth of Little League baseball was the contribution of the United States Rubber Company, now known as Uniroyal, spurred by an anticipated large market for kids' baseball shoes with rubberized spikes.

Before too long the Little League project had spread beyond Carl Stotz's grasp and the rubber company's executives took control of his idealistic dream. Ironically, when Stotz came to the realization that his original dream of baseball for boys had become a matter of corporate profit-and-loss, he withdrew his participation and decided to start again from scratch. Stotz toyed with the idea of forming a new league to be called the Original Little League, but the corporate powers-that-be filed suit against him. In essence, they prevented him from having anything to do with Little League baseball ever again. [2]

Putting Youth Sports in Perspective

Let's not put the entire rap on Little League baseball; when it comes to ultra-competitive parents and uninformed coaches, psychological horrors abound in all youth sports leagues.

George Welsh, the highly successful football coach at the University of Virginia, has long been a critic of youth league football. Welsh has gone on the record as saying that organized football for eight- and nine-year olds is just too demanding, both physically and emotionally. Even worse, he doesn't like the fact that young ballplayers become stereotyped at an early age. "A kid becomes a tackle at eight and he stays a tackle the rest of his life," observes Welsh. "How could that be much fun? At his age he should be learning all the skills. He should learn to throw and catch and run with the ball."

Welsh's comments are echoed by another Hall of Fame football name, Larry Csonka, a star running back at Syracuse and in the National Football League. Some football fans, aware of Csonka's rough-tough image, might be surprised to find that he didn't allow his two sons to play in midget football leagues.

Csonka observed about the youth football leagues in his neighborhood: "The coaches didn't know much about what they were doing. They just yelled a lot. They acted like they imagined Lombardi and Shula would act. Why, they had those eight-year-olds running gassers [long windsprints], for crying out loud."

Csonka continues: "The whole country loves football and so do I. But parents don't stop to consider all the things that can go wrong for a young fellow pushed into that kind of pressure. For one thing, he can come home with a handful of teeth. Worse, he can come home soured on athletics for life."[3]

Perhaps it shouldn't be surprising that it's the former professional athletes who so often step in and warn parents about letting their children play in organized youth leagues in which the coaching or supervising is out of sync with reality. After all, it's the professional athletes who have climbed that difficult pyramid of athletic success—and who knows better just what it takes to make it to the top of their profession?

But along with that competitive experience also comes lots of insight into the sport they "play." Galen Fiss used to play linebacker for the Cleveland Browns. One day in Kansas City, Fiss was coaching a youth football league when one of his lineman came out of the huddle hopping and skipping up to the line of scrimmage.

"For an instant our coaches were horrified," said Fiss. "That's not the way you're supposed to approach the line. But then we realized he's a ten-year-old kid! That's his way of having fun."[4]

The point is, rather than scream and yell at the little lineman to "get with it" and "look tough out there," Fiss and his coaching colleagues had the presence of mind to realize that the first priority in sports—as far as the kids are concerned—is having fun. Winning and losing are secondary, as that *USA Today* poll pointed out.

Stephen D. Ward never played professional football, but he did play college ball before going to medical school and ultimately becoming a psychiatrist. Highly respected and often cited in the psychiatric journals, Ward is fully aware of the impact that youth leagues have on our nation when it comes to producing future professional athletes. Dr. Ward writes "One hears claims that this or that number or percentage of professional baseball players got their first start in the Little League. But I am inclined to feel that they made it to the big leagues in spite of—rather than because of— their experience in the Little League."[5]

Keep Dr. Ward's comments in mind as you read through the following case studies.

Case Study #1: Mark Gubicza
Mark Gubicza has been one of the top American League pitchers over the last decade. Primarily with the Kansas City Royals, Gubicza (pronounced Goo-biz-ah) won 20 games for the Royals in 1988.

And yes, Mark is a product of Little League baseball, although the experience sticks in his mind to this day as an unpleasant one. Growing up in Philadelphia Mark was doubly blessed: not only was he considerably bigger than his peers when he was ten years old (he was already five feet three inches and weighed 110 pounds), but Mark was also a terrifically coordinated athlete.

But the parents of the other ten year olds didn't take kindly to Mark's God-given talents. Instead of praising him they intensely disliked Mark and resented his abilities. It got to the point that whenever Mark played ball in Little League, the parents from opposing teams would literally boo, curse, and scream at him.

Remember that Mark was all of ten years old. One afternoon Mark broke into tears while sitting on the bench. He eventually had to seek refuge and advice from his father, who was able to counsel Mark and help him look beyond all the booing and catcalling from the stands.

Fortunately for Gubicza, he and his dad were able to work through these problems. In fact, Mark had the rare ability to take all the negativity and jealousy aimed at him and use that energy to strengthen his determination to become the best athlete he could.

True, Mark Gubicza's story had a happy ending. But certainly there are thousands of other talented youngsters who weren't so fortunate. Their dreams and enjoyment of sports no doubt ended anonymously thanks to the boos and overly competitive environment of organized youth sports.

Case Study #2: Lee Guetterman

Like Mark Gubicza, Lee Guetterman was a top major league pitcher for several years. And like his counterpart with the Royals, Lee Guetterman also has very specific and disturbing memories of competing in an organized youth baseball league.

When Guetterman was twelve years old, he was thrilled to be selected for his league's all-star game. It was a big deal for Lee because the all-star selection was the first time he had ever been named to any kind of special team. The year before, when Lee was only eleven, he was a small, frail kid. Lee's coach didn't think he could help the team win so, as a result, Lee didn't play or pitch much that season.

But a year makes a big difference in a child's development. The day before the big all-star game, Lee Guetterman was talking about pitching with his coach. During the course of the conversation, the coach asked the twelve year old what he did to loosen his arm muscles up before he pitched. Understandably, Lee said he didn't do anything at all.

Horrified by this response, the all-star team coach told Lee that before pitching tomorrow he should take two aspirins and rub his pitching arm thoroughly with analgesic balm to keep the muscles warm and loose. Lee listened carefully to his coach and did exactly what he was told.

But the next day Lee went to the mound and found that his arm was so relaxed from the balm and aspirins that he had no strength in it whatsoever. Yet, rather than confront the coach, Lee dutifully went out, pitched as best as he could, and got hammered by the opposing team. It was a terrible day for the youngster, a day he still hasn't forgotten. Today Guetterman comments, "I learned from that experience that in order to prepare for a game I have to do what I know best. Coaches aren't always right. You have to discover for yourself what is right and wrong for you."

Case Study #3: Kevin Gross
Twelve-year-old Kevin Gross had a problem. He was the smallest, skinniest kid on his Little League team. Despite his diminutive size Kevin had great control and a terrific fastball. He was so good, in fact, that coaches from opposing teams always demanded to see his birth certificate because they were convinced he was much older.

Kevin, who has pitched for a number of major league teams, would always do his best despite the protests of the other teams. Looking back, Margot Gross, Kevin's mom, said, "How could you penalize a player for being too good? But that's what the opposing coaches were trying to do."

This story, like the first two, had a happy ending. Kevin Gross withstood all the negative competitive claims of opposing Little League coaches and eventually made it into the major league ranks.

A Word about Physical Size
The case study of Kevin Gross and his smallish size reinforces the point that kids grow at amazingly different rates.

Example: Diminutive pitcher Kevin Gross eventually grew up to be six-feet-five inches tall, and weigh over 200 pounds.

Example: Remember when Lee Guetterman was only eleven and was considered too small to help his team win? Little Lee now stands six-feet-eight inches tall and weighs 225.

Example: When ace relief pitcher John Franco of the New York Mets was a freshman in high school, he stood only five feet five inches and weighed less than a hundred pounds. His freshman coach took one look at John and told him to come back "when you've grown up."

It was nothing new to Franco, since he had always been the smallest kid on his Little League teams. But it wasn't until his sophomore year that Franco made his high school squad. And by the way, Franco now checks in at five-ten, 175 pounds.

A Word about Physical Development
As a parent/coach you might be tempted to expect greater skills from the physically larger athlete. Please understand that this expectation is simply wrong. In other words, just because one kid is physically larger than his or her friends, don't expect that particular child to be further developed in his or her athletic skills. It isn't fair to that child, to your child, or to yourself. Just remember the case studies above as a reminder of how young athletes mature at different speeds.

Not convinced? The great running back Herschel Walker, a terrific sprinter in college, couldn't beat his own sister in a footrace until he was 16 years old. And Michael Jordan didn't make his high school basketball team until his junior year![6]

Just How Important Is the Psychological Influence?
Very important—and you should never lose sight of the fact that while there are lots of really terrific youth sports coaches out there, there are also plenty of terrible ones. Some coaches can inflict emotional damage on your child without even being aware of it.

Literally dozens of psychological studies have confirmed that kids are in a very vulnerable situation when they play youth sports. Among the key findings:

- Strong evidence exists that children tend to form lifelong attitudes toward sports before they reach the age of ten.[7]

- That kids need the constant approval of coaches, and that they are much more sensitive to criticism than adults.[8]

- That an adult declaration of success or failure, of worthiness or unworthiness, is a major determinant of a child's self-esteem.[9]

- And perhaps most importantly, there are countless studies that indicate just how stressful the competition of youth sports can be for children—and just how detrimental that can be to their self-esteem. And who's providing most of the stress for the kids? That's right—the coaches and parents![10]

What Happens to Kids Who Are Stressed Out?

They give up. Or they turn away. Or they find some other nonathletic avocation to take up their time. Or they become depressed. You've heard of "burnout" among professional people such as doctors, social workers, and other individuals in high-pressure jobs. The same kind of thing often happens to children.

How does burnout occur? Too often the parents mistakenly assume that the child really wants to continue the sport in which he's shown promise and wants to continue that activity to the exclusion of other youth activities. A common example is the young boy or girl who shows tremendous promise in the swimming pool or as a tennis player or gymnast. Such promise can be exhibited as early as six or seven years of age.

But this athletic promise often confronts the adoring parents with a difficult decision: to let the child devote her full leisure time to that one particular sport (swimming, tennis, gymnastics, and so on) or to allow her to sample all kinds of sports that "little people" tend to enjoy?

For many parents this can be a real quandary. After all, tennis stars seem to get younger all the time; the same goes for Olympic swimmers and gymnasts. But more and more psychologists point out the dangers of having a child devote all of his or her spare time to just one athletic pursuit at an early age. Imagine what must go through an eight-year-old's mind when he is told by Mom and Dad that "if he wants to become the best in his chosen sport, then he'll have to swim dozens of laps in a pool day after day." That's kind of a tough sentence for a youngster who just wants to have fun. But the tragedy is that it happens every day all over the country.

Whenever you find yourself worrying about a child's dedication to just one sport, keep in mind a classic book on athletics entitled, *The Pursuit of Sporting Excellence.* David Hemery, an Olympic hurdler, interviewed 63 of the world's greatest athletes about their development in sports. In his results he found that only five of these great athletes ever specialized in just one sport before the age of twelve, and that the average age of one-sport specialization for these athletes was sixteen.

One of those athletes who didn't specialize in a particular sport until he was sixteen was Carl Lewis, the world-class sprinter and jumper. Grant Hill, the star of the Detroit Pistons, was a terrific soccer player into his teens before deciding to concentrate on hoops. And NBA All-Star Hakeem Olajuwon didn't start playing until he was 18![11]

What happens to children who do specialize at a very young age? At the very least many of them end up experiencing burnout. And at the other end of the spectrum, many simply miss out on the normal developmental patterns of childhood, such as making friends, enjoying creative games, and trying out other sporting activities.

You've seen all the magazine and television reports about the next young tennis star or Olympic hopeful. And chances are you've asked yourself, "I wonder why the parent pushes that child so hard?" The answers are numerous, but more often than not, there is usually an underlying adult drive that's pushing that little person's need to achieve and to win.

According to a widely quoted study, one psychologist has concluded: "Adult egos too often turn the game into a victory drive or a training ground for future stars with their children as pawns."[12]

Children's Experiences
The point is, parents must come to grips with the simple reality that a child's perspective on sports and games is much, much different from that of an adult. As George F. Will, the well-known columnist and author of the best-selling book *Men at Work,* points out, "Children are an enlarging if sobering experience, and often amusing. But childhood is frequently a solemn business for those inside it."

To Will and many parents, it is clear that children take their play very seriously. They ought to be wary that in the context of youth league play, their children don't take it too seriously. Whereas the adult can usually put winning and losing into proper perspective in the scope of life, a child is still grappling with those abstract concepts. And unless those concepts are placed into a proper philosophical framework, the realities of winning and losing can be skewed way out of proportion for the youngster.

The famous developmental psychologist Erik Erikson pointed out that from the ages of seven through 12 children are constantly learning about their worldly environment. During this time they are driven to master certain skills and roles in their daily world. They are constantly overcoming feelings of inferiority (ever notice how a child will keep practicing a skill over and over again until he or she perfects it?). And when kids do master a certain skill, they feel proud of their own personal accomplishment.

Of course, a major driving force in this pursuit of mastery comes from a desire to please one's parents. Parental approval is very significant in this period of a child's existence.

But what parents look upon as "simple child's play" is to the child a very serious matter. Too often parents forget that—a particularly common failing when a parent pushes a youngster into one sport at too early an age.

Imagine—how would you like to spend all your time doing only one activity? How much fun would that be for you? Imagine how your child would enjoy the same kind of experience.

The "Has-Been" Syndrome
There are other common syndromes for young athletes as well. Perhaps the opposite of the burnout syndrome—the case of a kid who plays one sport too much—is the child who doesn't get to play enough—the so-called "has-been" who never "was."

In some ways this is an even more dangerous and tragic situation than that of the burnout victim.

- According to a recent study, as many as 80 percent of all children who play youth sports drop out of competitive sports by the time they reach the ripe old age of 12.[13]

- In Canada, where ice hockey is practically a religion, you might be surprised to learn that according to a Canadian Amateur Hockey Association poll of a few years ago, there were 600,000 players registered with the CAHA, of whom 53 percent were under the age of 12; 35 percent were between 12 and 15; and only 11 percent were over the age of 15. In other words, by age 15 only about one out of every ten kids in Canada is actually playing youth ice hockey. And there is every indication that similar percentages apply to kids in the United States in such sports as baseball, football, and soccer. [14]

Why do these trends exist? Because sometime during their early sporting careers, too many of these kids had the misfortune to have fallen into the hands of coaches who decided that they weren't good enough to play. Subsequently, these kids decided it wasn't fun anymore.

Even worse, too many coaches just flat out decide that they want to "show kids that sports can be a positive experience—but that it can only be positive if they play on a winning team." Hence, the coach plays the more advanced players most of the time while the less talented kids play limited amounts. From the coach's point of view, the "lesser" kids share in their teammates' on-the-field successes.

You can imagine how much fun it must be for an eight-year-old to always be in the position of having to congratulate his teammates for playing well while he's relegated to the role of bench reserve. It doesn't take a Ph.D. in psychology to figure out that if a child doesn't get to play much, after a while he won't show much enthusiasm for signing up the next year.

In other words, the eight year old who may just be a bit small in size or who hasn't had much practice in a particular sport is shut out of the enjoyment of the sport; he has, in essence, become a "has-been" before being given a chance to develop his skills.

Judging from the statistics cited above, for four out of five young athletes the trend seems to be away from competitive sports in their teens.

Competition—an Evil?

Not at all. In fact, competition is the essence of any sporting endeavor. Indeed, organized youth sports should serve as the introduction to healthy competition. But introduction is the operative word here since kids react to competition in various ways.

Carolyn W. Sherif, one of the nation's leading psychologists, once wrote that "ordinarily, by about the age of six in our society, a child can and does compete. Still, the consistency of competitive behaviors varies enormously." What Dr. Sherif means by this is that just as kids develop at different rates physically, they also develop their sense of competitiveness at different rates as well. It's up to the coach/adult/parent to determine how much competition a child can absorb without damaging his fragile sense of self-esteem. [15]

Do not take this assessment lightly, because the child's view of competition is carried over from the playing fields into the classroom. In his classic work, *How Children Fail,* noted educator and author John Holt recognized back in the 1960s that in the typical classroom setting, most children are scared and intimidated at the thought of failing in class. Rather than compete against their peers in the classroom, they tend to be afraid, bored, or confused. In essence they turn away from the free spirit of academic competition.

Ideally, one wants children to perform in the classroom and on the playing fields simply because they are motivated by the pure joy of mastering a new skill. The last thing parents want is for their child to hold back from new challenges in the classroom or in sports; this kind of intimidation is based upon a fear of failing rather than the pure pleasure of spontaneous play.

Spontaneous Play

One of the gravest concerns that psychologists have about organized youth leagues is that because they are set up by adults, run by adults, and maintained by adults, they tend to overlook the spontaneous needs and desires of young children. Experts in child development, dating back to Jean Piaget, have long noted that kids like to fantasize and fabricate the "rules" of their games as they play them. You have seen your own child engage in a playful fantasy land in which he or she is "lost" in conversation with playthings or imaginary playmates. This kind of spontaneous play is the stuff of creativity and tends to fuel the child's enjoyment of her own games.

Indeed, because these spontaneous games are played on a plane of fantasy, the so-called "realistic consequences" of winning or losing are never even considered a risk. That's a vital consideration for the child, because for her, the act of playing is supposed to be fun and of no risk at all.

But as soon as the concept of "rules" and the idea of "victory or defeat" are injected into the child's mind, much of the simplistic, refreshing spontaneity vanishes. After all, there's no time to fantasize about one's play when one is being judged according to "the rules of the game,"—a game usually set up by (you guessed it) parents.

Does this mean that without the interference or leadership of parents, kids would never learn the rules of a sport? Not at all. Piaget pointed out that from his observations, kids when left to their own devices will ultimately develop their own rules of fair play and competitive right and wrong. Piaget pointed out that if several children are left to play with marbles, eventually they will figure out on their own how to develop a sense of equitable play. In effect, learning the rules of fair play is critical not only to the child's sense of creative spontaneity, but also to her moral growth and the development of social cooperation. [16]

Lawrence Kohlberg, another noted psychologist who specializes in moral development, points out that if children are simply taught arbitrary rules without ever understanding why they have evolved, they will learn the dogma of the rules without any moral experience. If a sense of fair play and sportsman ship is an important value for a parent to impart to a child, then the child should experience why rules evolve the way they do.

What does all this mean in terms of the young athlete? Edward C. Devereux, a psychologist at Cornell University concludes:

> In Little League ball the spontaneity is largely killed by schedules, rules, and adult supervision—a fixed time and place for each game, a set number of innings, a commitment to a whole season's schedule at the expense of alternative activities. Self-pacing? Obviously not. Fun? Yes, in a hard sort of way; but, please, no fooling around or goofing off out there in right field; keep your eyes on the ball! Instant feedback? Yes, loud and clear from all sides, if you make a mistake; but mostly from adults, in terms of their criteria of proper baseball performance.

> The major problem with Little League baseball, as I see it, is that the whole structure of the game is rigidly fixed once and for all. It's all there in the rule books and in the organization of the League and the game itself.... Almost all the opportunities for incidental learning which occur in spontaneous self organized and self-governed children's games have somehow been sacrificed on the altar of safety (physical only) and competence (in baseball only).[17]

Competitive Anxiety in Kids

Recently, a mother who doesn't really follow sports asked me what a "game face" was, because her son always seemed to become extremely nervous and agitated the night before a baseball game.

When I asked her to relate in what context she had heard the expression, she answered that her son's coach had used it. Specifically, she said that she had asked the coach about her son being so tense and nervous before a game. He had brushed her worries aside, remarking that he "was only putting on his game face."

In sports parlance a "game face" is the sign of an athlete's complete concentration on an upcoming game. His usual pleasant manners go by the wayside, replaced by brooding self-absorption. In most cases this "game face" mentality disappears right after the game. But the concern for parents, as this particular mom asked, is "Why does a player even need a game face? It seems to me that he should be looking forward to having fun; instead, he's terribly worried about how he's going to do."

Indeed, she's absolutely correct. A game face is the outward manifestation of an athlete's anxiety. While that gnawing worry might be acceptable for a professional or college-age athlete, it certainly doesn't make sense for a youngster.

The point is simple: If the young athlete constantly feels threatened, nervous, or anxious about his performance, why does he continue to pursue the sport in question? In many ways the anxiety a youngster feels about game day is similar to what he experiences when he has to go to the dentist, take a big test, or deliver a speech in school.

Kids tend to deal with stress in various ways. Some, for example, bite their fingernails out of worry. I once worked with a top college All-American baseball player who got so nervous before games that he not only bit his nails to the quick, he would literally chew all the hair off his fingers and wrists. (And mind you, he was an All-American!)

Other kids throw up before a big game. Some literally pee in their pants. Many are too nervous to eat or sleep. They get headaches. Or they get so wound up that they can't concentrate on anything else in their life, including school.

A few years ago the pulse rate of Little Leaguers was taken at various intervals during the course of a game. While they were on the bench before the game, the average pulse rate was 97 beats a minute. But once the game began, the kids' rates averaged 127 beats per minute. And when they came to bat, their pulse raced all the way to 167 beats per minute. In fact, one kid's rate raced all the way to 204 beats a minute when batting. [18]

So Sports Cause Stress ... So What?

"Okay, okay," you're saying, "I know that kids can get overexcited and perhaps overstressed about a big game. I know that and I know my kid."

But *do* you? One of the more distressing psychological studies revealed a very scary analysis of stress in kids. Specifically, in one study that focused on female coaches of youth athletes, it turned out that the vast majority were terrible predictors of stress in children. In fact, the coaches could accurately predict the athletes' anxiety in fewer than 10 percent of the kids on their teams. And by the way—these were not volunteer or amateur coaches, but trained, professional coaches at the high school and collegiate level. [19]

The Coach: Sacrificing the Win

For the youth league coach who takes his sport too seriously, the idea of making victory a second priority to the enjoyment of the game is not only a foreign concept, it's downright treasonous.

But if the coach really understands and accepts that for kids playing is more fun than winning or losing, then he is on his way to making the season a productive and enjoyable one for all the kids on the squad, one in which each child will have an equal amount of playing time and that will, according to the sport, enable them to play different positions.

That, of course, is the fundamental purpose of youth sports: to allow the children to learn and enjoy a sport without the anxiety of having to keep score or care about winning or losing. If the coach your child plays for truly embraces this concept, you can rest assured that your child has a good chance of having a lot of fun this season.

As Lao Tse, the famous Chinese philosopher once observed: "If you tell me, I will listen. If you show me, I will see. If you let me experience it, I will learn."

Who's Keeping Score?

In the early years of youth sports, there is absolutely no reason to keep score of the games. This includes youth sports from ages six through nine. After age nine, the kids themselves begin to fully comprehend the meaning of competition, and score becomes a more meaningful part of the game to them.

But in the early years, score is kept more for the parents' egos than for the kids. Since kids can hardly even figure out the rules of most sports before the age of nine, it's kind of silly to keep score. Also, if all the coaches in the league really decide to put the kids' fun ahead of winning and losing, then scorekeeping becomes even less meaningful.

Yet each season there's going to be at least one coach who takes the score of the games very, very seriously. He'll protest every controversial call, he'll want his kids to go out to win every game, and he'll do whatever he can to ensure victory for his team. In essence, he'll have his list of priorities upside down.

If your child happens to be on this coach's team, be diplomatic, but strong-willed, about your feelings. Let the coach know early on that you protest. You don't have to make a big scene out of it or get into a shouting match. Just let the coach know in a quiet, one-to-one conversation that your child is not going to benefit from this kind of coaching environment.

If the coach doesn't change his style, then it's up to you to protest to the league's ruling body. And if they don't want to help you out or place your child on another coach's team, then it's up to you to take a stand and either rally and organize the other parents or simply remove your child from that youth sports league.

No, you won't win any popularity contests in your neighborhood. But if you want to do what's right for your child, you'll do whatever it takes to guarantee that competitive sports are kept in proper perspective.

A few years ago a couple of psychologists recommended the following guidelines for youth sports. Even though they may sound a bit unorthodox to you, they're worth bearing in mind:

- All score books should be eliminated.

- Let the players select their coaches and let them umpire or referee their own games.

- Let each player play the same amount of time.

- Don't be afraid not to enforce a rule if it gets in the way of the kids' playing.[20]

In other words, if you let your top priority be the children's amusement and the sheer fun of playing the sport, you'll ensure that they're keeping their priorities straight as well. Surely you have heard the old sports maxim, "It's not whether you win or lose, but how you play the game."

As far as kids are concerned, that particular phrase carries more truth than most parents imagine. One telltale study proves exactly that point. In 1974 a landmark study on children in sports asked these questions:

- Would you rather play simply for fun, or would you prefer to win?

- Would you rather be on a winning team but sit on the bench, or would you rather play a lot on a team that loses a lot?

The results shouldn't surprise you. Over 95 percent of the kids replied that they would rather simply have fun than worry about winning, and over 90 percent said they would prefer to be on a losing team if they were able actually to play in the games rather than be bench warmers on a winning team.[21]

The results are clear: On the whole kids would rather simply play and have fun. Too often, it's the adults who get in the way of their fun and enjoyment.

1. *Newsweek*, July 21, 1975.
2. Martin Ralbovsky, *Lords of the Locker Room* (New York: Wyden Books, 1974), p. 121.
3. Rainer Martens, *Joy and Sadness in Children's Sports* (Champaign, Ill.: Human Kinetics Publishers, 1978), p. 54.
4. Ibid., p. 58.
5. Ibid., p. 76.
6. Nate Zinsser, *Dear Dr. Psych* (New York: Time-Warner Inc., 1991), p. 36.
7. D. Pease and D. Anderson, "Longitudinal Analysis of Children's Attitudes toward Sport Team Involvement," *Journal of Sport Behavior*, Vol. 9, pp. 3-10, 1986.
8. J. Fowler, *Movement Education* (Philadelphia: Saunders College Publishing, 1981). See also: B. Cratty, *Psychology in Contemporary Sport: Guidelines for Coaches and Athletes*, 2nd ed . (Englewood Cliffs, N.J.: Prentice-Hall, 1983).
9. L. Hilgers, "Stress-Free Little League," *Sports Illustrated*, August 22, 1988, pp. 90-91.
10. B. Lombardo, "The Behavior of Youth Sport Coaches: Crisis on the Bench," *Arena Review*, Vol. 6, pp. 48-55, 1982. See also: R. Smith and F. Smoll, "Psychological Stress: A Conceptual Model and Some Intervention Strategies in Youth Sports," pp. 178-195, in *Children in Sport: A Contemporary Anthology* (Champaign, Ill.: Human Kinetics Publishers, 1982).
11. Nate Zinsser, *Dear Dr. Psych*, op. cit., p. 61.
12. J. Brower, "The Professionalization of Organized Youth Sports," *Annals of AAPSS*, Vol. 445, pp. 39-46, 1979.
13. G. Roberts, "The Growing Child and the Perception of Competitive Stress in Sport" in *The Growing Child in Competitive Sport*, ed. G. Gleeson (London: Hodder and Stoughton, 1986), pp. 130-144.
14. T. Orlick, *Every Kid Can Win* (Chicago: Nelson-Hall, Inc., 1975).
15. C. Sherif, *Orientation in Social Psychology* (HarperCollins, New York, 1976).
16. J. Piaget, *The Moral Judgment of the Child* (New York: Harcourt Brace, 1932).
17. E. Devereux, "Backyard versus Little League Baseball," *Social Problems in Athletics* (Champaign, Ill.: University of Illinois Press, 1976), pp. 37-56.
18. D. Hanson, "Cardiac Response to Participation in Little League Baseball Competition as Determined by Telemetry," *Research Quarterly*, Vol. 38, pp. 384-388, 1968.
19. R. Martens and J. Simon, "Comparison of Three Predictors of State Anxiety in Competitive Situations, " *Research Quarterly*, Vol. 47, pp. 381-387, 1976.
20. L. Yablonsky and J. Brower, *The Little League Game* (New York: Times Books, 1979).
21. T. Orlick, "The Athletic Dropout—a High Price for Inefficiency, " *Canadian Association for Health, Physical Education and Recreation Journal*, Sept/Oct. 1974, pp. 21-27.

CHAPTER 3

Reports from the Field

I'm sure you've heard the expression "Kill the ump!" Fortunately, most baseball fans use it only in the most figurative way.

Yet, in the spring of 1991, the police in East St. Louis, Illinois were forced to arrest one angry Little League coach who felt that the umpire had made a wrong call during a game played by nine-year olds. According to the official police reports, the angered coach's team was losing by one run when there was a close play at home plate and the potential tying run was called out. Furious over the call, the coach grabbed a bat and charged the 16-year-old umpire. Among his threats, the coach told the umpire that he would bust his head and kill him.

After the coaches from the other team rescued the ump, the enraged coach stomped off in a fit but returned about ten minutes later with a handgun. The coach stopped within ten feet of the umpire, who was still working the game on the field, and fired several rounds at him. Miraculously the ump escaped without being hit. [1]

- In Virginia a softball umpire made a tough call and was rewarded for his decision by having one of the fans pull out a .357-caliber handgun and threaten him on the spot. The action took place in a girls' organized softball league, ages eight to eleven.[2]

- Jo-Ann Allard of Newington, Connecticut, was enjoying watching her nine-year-old son, Peter, play in an organized youth football league last fall when she heard another mother yell out to one of the kids, "You see that number twenty-four? I want to see blood on your helmet!"

  Allard was stunned; number 24 was her son, Peter. She turned to the other mother who was standing a few feet away, and said, "Hey, that's my son you're talking about."

  The other mom simply fired back, "Look, lady, we're playing football here."[3]

- Russell Karkheck, a psychologist based in Pomona, New York, tells the story of how one father and son reacted to Little League pressure. Although the child showed great promise as a pitcher, he preferred to throw sidearm rather than in the conventional overhand style.

  Recalls Karkheck: "The boy's father felt that if he continued to throw sidearm, he could develop arm trouble. The father actually considered putting his son's arm in a cast at a right angle so that the boy would learn to throw overhand."[4]

The problem with stories like these is that there are just too many to keep up with. Indeed, one could fill an entire volume with abuses from youth sports.

- In an effort to "motivate" his players for a big game, a Little League coach in California burned the uniform of the opposing team in effigy in front of his own ballclub.

- Fights among opposing coaches are so routine as to be reported in the newspapers only if one of the coaches is seriously injured. Shouting matches between coaches are no longer considered news worth reporting.

- Even worse the number of officials, referees, and umpires who are attacked for "poor officiating" by youth league parents and coaches continues to grow every year. In fact, Mel Narol, an attorney practicing in Princeton, New Jersey, devotes his entire law practice to representing these injured officials in court—and he's never been busier.

- There are countless reports of preteens ingesting diet pills in order to stay under a certain weight so as to be eligible for youth football and wrestling leagues. There are endless accounts of parents who lie about their kids' ages so that their kids qualify for youth league age requirements. And there are the stories in every community in which one coach runs the kids' team as though he's the head coach of the Chicago Bears. He's the guy who tends to espouse the philosophy, "Kids only have fun when they win. If they don't win, what fun can it be?"

The More Subtle—and More Common—Forms of Abuse

Okay, I'll admit that several of the above examples were selected to illustrate just how extreme off-base parental intervention can become in youth sports. You're probably saying, "Sure, we've got some nutty coaches in our town, but nobody would ever pull a gun on an umpire."

You're probably right. But as you have read, emotional abuse in organized youth sports leagues can take many forms. And while it may not be as dramatic as firing a gun at an umpire, chances are you have either experienced or witnessed other more subtle but psychologically distressing forms of coaching abuse with your kids.

For openers, have you ever seen any of the following "coaching strategies" in use in your youth leagues?

- The coach of one of the teams very subtly works at "stacking" his team with the very best players in the league.

- The coach of your child's team plays his or her own son or daughter in every game in the most desirable field position while the other kids rotate in and out of the lineup.

- The coach tells the kids on the team that to be fair they will get playing time based strictly upon how good they are.

- The coach uses profanity and obscene language whenever he or she feels like it, either during a practice session or during a game.

- The coach doesn't interfere if any of the kids start teasing each other or start having fights among themselves, taking the attitude that "kids will be kids."

- The coach constantly harasses and harangues the referee, umpire, or official who is working the game.

- The coach sees nothing wrong with yelling and screaming at his or her players if they aren't playing well.

- The coach insists that his or her players practice only those skills that the coach wants and in only the manner the coach wants them practiced (e.g., a child wants to adopt a certain batting stance while the coach insists the child change his or her style).

- The coach smokes cigars, cigarettes, chews tobacco, or drinks alcohol during the course of a game or practice.

Stacking one's team is perhaps the best-known violation of youth sports leagues ethics. It's become so epidemic throughout the country that it's the rare youth league in which the practice doesn't take place. But, of course, there are many varieties of coaching abuse in youth sports.

There's the coach who makes certain his or her child gets the most playing time and is rewarded with the best position on the field as though he or she is the best player on the team—even when he or she isn't. Or perhaps your son or daughter has had to put up with a coach who "teaches discipline the old-fashioned way"— usually by means of harsh language with a drill sergeant's sense of compassion.

Maybe you've seen your child's coach become so obsessed with winning that he or she plays the more talented children for the majority of the game—then lets the "lesser" kids play once the score of the game is lopsided. The point is, if you've ever let your child participate in these leagues, you know firsthand that there are lots of things you would probably change.

Within my own community in a soccer league for six and seven year olds, I have witnessed these kinds of disturbing behavior patterns routinely. One spring I saw a fist-fight break out between two opposing coaches. I heard a coach yell at his team that they "could win this game only if they wanted victory so bad they could taste it." I've seen a referee whose son or daughter was playing in the game—and losing— allow the running time of the game to go on and on until his child's team tied the game up. And one time, when I was personally refereeing a game, I was bitterly confronted by a father who berated me over and over with obscenities for not having called an off-sides.

Again, this was in a soccer league for six- and seven-year-olds. Most kids at that age can hardly tell right from left, much less understand the subtleties of an off-sides call.

What does one do in these kinds of situations? Rest assured that we will deal with many of these perplexing questions later in the book. But the first concern here is for the parent to at least become aware of these kinds of problems.

Of course, if you are of the opinion—like the coach above—that "kids will be kids" when it comes to youth sports, then this book is going to be of little use to you. But if you are concerned about such pressures being applied to your son or daughter or if you are concerned that your child's enjoyment of a sport is dissipating due to the highly competitive atmosphere of an organized youth league, then it's up to you to become involved in what's going on. After all, you wouldn't hesitate for a moment if you felt your child's teacher was doing something terribly wrong in the classroom so why should you allow his or her coach to do something just as wrong on the athletic field?

A good friend of mine is a physician who also happens to have a very talented son who is a stand out ice hockey player. The boy, who is ten years old, plays for a youth hockey team. Although it's apparent that my friend's son loves the sport and is good on the ice, the coach of his team doesn't seem to give him much playing time.

When I asked my friend about this situation and how frustrating it must be for his son, as well as for himself, he simply shrugged his shoulders and said, "I don't think it would be right for me to get involved. After all, I don't want to get labeled as a meddling father. Besides, it's probably a good experience for my son to play for both good and not-so-good coaches."

I was stunned when I heard this answer, but upon reflection, perhaps I shouldn't have been; it's typical of the answers most parents would give.

Yet, think of the ironies. If the child does enjoy the sport and even shows a talent for it, don't you owe it to him at least to find out from the coach why he doesn't get as much playing time as the others? And as for the rationale that he has to get used to playing for both good and bad coaches, let's remember that if the child happens to have the misfortune of having bad coaches early in his playing career, there's a good chance his playing career will only last a few years. Why? Because he played for a lousy coach who took the fun and pleasure out of playing that sport!

Common sense? Perhaps. But how many parents go to watch their sons and daughters play on a youth league team, say practically nothing to the coach, and then go home in their station wagon muttering to themselves about why the coach doesn't let their son or daughter play more or try a more desirable position? And they go through the same experience the following Saturday when the next game pops up on the schedule.

Good Coaches Are Essential

Look, I've played for both good and bad coaches in my athletic career. As you might imagine, almost all of the coaches in my early years were supportive, caring people; otherwise, I would never have kept playing sports into my college years. It's simple logic. If your kids don't enjoy sports when they're young, they sure won't be tempted to keep playing them as they get older.

It might surprise parents of Little Leaguers to learn that the way in which Little League is set up, it's not always the best team that goes to the championship. That is, the system rewards only the best individual players rather than the entire winning team, and compiles an all-star team of all the best League players for the championship game. Therefore, from the first game of the season, Little League coaches are scouting for the best players in the league.

This practice runs totally counter to the concept of play first and worry about winning second. In 1989 in Dale City, Virginia, some 16 less-than-spectacularly-talented kids were placed on a "waiting list" in the hopes that a Little League team within their community might select them. In effect, they were forced to sit out most of the season, even though the Official Regulations and Playing Rules of Little League specify that all kids who are old enough are eligible to play and should get at least one at-bat a game and two innings in the field per game.

Vern Seefeldt, Director of the Michigan Youth Sports Institute, comments : "The tournament structure [of Little League] eliminates players, and it promotes the elitism of a select few players." In response to that charge, Dr. Creighton Hale, the president of Little League, says, "The Little League World Series is just the frosting on the cake, in which the most highly skilled youngsters get to compete. If we're not concerned about the other 2.5 million youngsters, something's wrong."[5]

Where Does the Fun Come In?

Jay Feldman, a freelance writer and father from Woodland, California writes:

> Recently my wife and I were watching our nine-year-old son's Little League game when she turned to me and said, "There's something missing here, but I'm not sure what it is." I knew what she meant, but I couldn't put my finger on it.

That weekend my son accompanied me to my over-30 baseball team's practice. There were a few other kids there, and we gave them a bat and ball and sent them to the other end of the park. Very soon the exuberant sounds from their game caught my ear. I looked over, and at the sight of them leaping and frisking unselfconsciously about, I knew at once what had been missing from that Little League game—the spontaneous, unrestrained exhilaration of kids having fun.[6]

His point is well taken. Remember that kids play and enjoy sports—or for that matter any game—for the sheer joy of being in a free, fantasy-like environment. There is no risk, no sense of urgency, no sense of fear, only the pure fun of meeting and mastering a challenge. It could be as simple as hitting a tennis ball over a net, or swimming across a pool, or walking across a balance beam. Or it could be a bit more sophisticated, such as playing against a childhood opponent in a soccer game, pick-up baseball game, or basketball game.

What Jay Feldman points out is that there is a fundamental difference between watching kids play at large on a playground with no adult supervision and what happens to kids when they don uniforms, look up at the scoreboard, and have to perform for their parents.

On a playground you hear kids laugh, shout, and show all the signs of pure play or fun. But on a soccer field or baseball diamond or in any other youth sports league, you rarely hear the sounds of laughter. Rather, you hear coaches barking out orders and parents exhorting their children to win.

In other words, one environment is fun, as evidenced by the laughter. The other environment is a cauldron in which a child's competitive skills are tested—with the child hoping and praying for the best.

> Ask yourself—which kind of environment do you want for your son or daughter?

George Mercerod is a former professional pitcher who spent nine years playing in the Boston Red Sox organization and for the White Sox and the Cubs. But when Mercerod brought his five-year-old son, Michael, out to Pee-Wee baseball practice in Commack, Long Island, he was stunned to be told by the league's director that he shouldn't pitch the ball to the kids who were taking batting practice.

Mercerod recalls:

> He came over to me and told me that this was a league based solely for tee-ball, and that there was no room for pitching. I simply explained to him that while tee-ball was fine and that I understood the concept behind it, I also felt that if the kids wanted to hit off a pitcher, then they should be entitled to do so.
>
> The director told me that pitching takes too long, because the kids can't hit, and because of that, it would take too much time. Practice would take too long. I asked him, "Why don't we let the kids decide what they want to do? After all, it's their league and their practice."
>
> Well, he looked at me like I was nuts, like "Let the kids decide? What a crazy idea!" But I tell you what. The kids really did like hitting my underhanded tosses, and that's the way we ended up playing for the rest of the spring. By the time we were finished, they were learning how to become good hitters.

The Age-Old "Do-Over"

Here's another thought about spontaneous play between kid- and adult-run organized youth sports leagues. When kids at play have a dispute, either about the game, each other, or a play, they quickly learn the age-old concept of the "do-over," as in "Let's do the play over again."

This is not to be overlooked, because the do-over is a vital process of social compromise and acceptance. It's more than just the experience of coping with frustration in a game; it's part of learning an important social skill.

But something curious happens to the concept of the "do-over" once you mix in the parent/adult element in youth leagues. When you have refs, umpires, or officials, the supervising adults make the final and unchallengeable call and the kids abide with that decision for better or worse. (If there is a dispute over the call, usually it's the kids' coaches or parents who make the big stink—not the kids themselves.)

But more importantly, the kids have totally skipped the experience of the "do-over" and everything that social skill means in terms of coping with and adapting to their friends and colleagues. As many child experts point out, learning the "do-over" concept is practically the first step in a child's learning the fundamentals of fair play and sportsmanship.

Trust Your Child's Instincts

One of the more curious aspects of youth sports is that parents often don't give their children enough credit for having common sense and the ability to put things in perspective. While it may be true that kids are learning the fundamentals of sports while in their very early years, they also learn quickly about competition and fair play.

- For example, kids are adept at quickly figuring out who among their peers is a good sport and who isn't. As part of that national survey that was reported in *USA Today*, kids were much more adept at pointing out "poor sports" among their colleagues than were their observing parents.

- Curiously, of the parents surveyed, only 59 percent mentioned "having fun" as the top priority for their children. Close to 70 percent of the kids of those very same parents put "having fun" as their first priority.

- Even more interesting was that when the parents were asked to rate their children's coaches, only 19 percent of the coaches were rated as being "excellent." Fifty-five percent were rated as being only "good." But disturbingly, 22 percent of the kids' coaches were evaluated as being "fair" and 3 percent as "poor." That means, according to this recent survey, that one of every four youth coaches is less than good, as seen by the parents. No matter how you view that, it's not a particularly encouraging score.

Be an Active Listener

As intriguing as survey results can be, the best way to discover how much your child is getting out of his or her involvement in an organized youth league is simply to listen. As a parent you want to know how your child is doing in school, and periodically you get report cards from your child's teacher. And while you won't receive a report card on your child from his or her coach, you can certainly speak to your son or daughter at appropriate quiet times to find out just how much they're enjoying the experience. Be an active listener when your child speaks to you about sports.

Some of the basic questions you might want to ask your child to get you started include:

- "Are you looking forward to the game on Saturday?"

This is usually an easy way to start a conversation about the sport that your child is playing. Normally, the child will tell you that he can't wait for the game. Obviously, if he indicates that he could care less or hadn't thought about it much or really doesn't want to think about it, those are signs that your child isn't enjoying the experience or is perhaps too young (at five or six years old) to understand the excitement of anticipating a game.

But if real signs of apathy exist, you might want to consider your child's involvement on the team. True, some parents believe strongly that "once my child makes a commitment to a team, then it's up to him or her to follow through on that commitment." But if your child is only five or six or seven, the concept of team commitment is likely still very foreign to him. Making him attend all those practice sessions and games is not going to teach him anything about "commitment"; rather, it's most likely going to turn him off from the sport.

Don't get me wrong—the concept of commitment to a team is certainly important, but it shouldn't be pressed on a child until the age of at least eight.

- "Do you enjoy playing on the team, or would you rather just play with your friends in the neighborhood?"

This is an excellent opportunity to judge whether or not your child is really enjoying the experience. After all, she already knows how enjoyable playing with her friends is. You're simply asking her to compare that fun with the fun of playing on a team.

Again, if she can't decide, or if she feels that playing with her friends is more fun, then take that as a signal to reconsider her involvement with the youth league.

And don't worry about her being "left behind" when it comes to team sports. If she doesn't enjoy being on the team, then she's not going to benefit much from the experience anyhow. Better to let her have fun and build self-confidence on her own.

- "Is the coach nice to you?"

An important question, and it's important to leave this question open-ended. Even if you attend every practice session and every game, chances are that you don't know for sure whether or not your child responds in a positive, warm way to the coach, is fearful of the coach, or is afraid to do anything wrong for fear of being reprimanded or scolded.

Always bear in mind that most kids do whatever it takes to please Mom and Dad, or their coaches and teachers. Hence, there's a major difference between a child who tells you that "the coach says I have to work harder to get better" and the child who says, "He's the best—he's going to let me play goalie next game!"

On one hand, as a parent, you're pleased that your child is learning that he has to practice more to play better. But that's like telling a kid that he has to brush his teeth and drink his milk. Sure, he'll respond to that demand, but only because he wants to please the coach or you. On the other hand, when a kid beams with enthusiasm that he can't wait for the next game, then you know that his motivation for the game comes from the anticipation of pure fun as opposed to a simple desire to please the coach or you.

- "How important is winning to you?"

For many kids, especially at the younger ages, this question really won't mean much. But when your child begins to reach the age of eight or nine, he knows well what winning and losing mean. The question then is one that's worth pondering, because everybody prefers to win—that's a given.

But what about losing? Ideally, you want your child simply to come home from a game thinking, no matter what the final outcome, I had fun and I did my best. But that's an ideal situation and it rarely happens. In fact, many times a loss will bring tears of sadness and frustration. It's important for you and the coach to respond in an appropriate manner.

In terms of the coach, while everyone acknowledges that losing is part of sports, the problem is that people react to it in different ways. In youth organized sports make an effort to see how your son or daughter's coach reacts to a loss then watch how the coach allows the kids to react. Obviously, if the coach is distraught or yelling at the ref or the kids, you know you've got a problem. At the other extreme, you don't want the coach to brush off the loss without even acknowledging it.

When I work with seven- and eight-year-olds after a soccer game they have just lost, I bring the team together, get their attention, and while I dole out lots of praise for their effort and play, I also point out to them that winning and losing are part of all sporting ventures, and that it's very important for an athlete to be both a kind winner and a gracious loser.

The Art of Winning—and Losing

This is where sportsmanship begins at this early age. Certainly, you want your child to play hard and have fun and even to win. But once the game is over, it's time to put the rivalry to rest and to congratulate the winners and console the losers. And it's up to you, the adult/parent, to set a good example.

How does one set a good example? Simple. By keeping your emotions under control. Don't allow yourself to become too ecstatic when your child wins and more importantly, don't become too depressed if your child loses. Some parents become downright angry when their child loses or doesn't play well, and the trip home in the family car becomes solemn and funereal.

Then during that long ride home, the accusations begin to pour out of the parent's mouth:

- "I thought I told you how to make that play...."

- "Didn't we practice that situation all week? What happened in the game?"

- "You know, if you had simply scored that goal, we would have tied the game instead of lost...."

- "What was wrong with you today? Didn't you feel like playing hard?"

- "I feel sorry for you, because you aren't on a very good team...."

- "It's a good thing your coach is a nice guy, because if I were your coach, I would never stand for that kind of behavior...."

- "If you're going to play the game, you might as well win. That's what sports are all about...."

Remarks like these are made all the time. What's surprising is that these alarming comments may come out of the mouths of the most caring and decent of parents.

But parents are adults, and because adults tend to speak to others, including their own kids, on an adult basis, they quickly fall into this trap of criticizing a child's performance on grown-up terms.

For a kid, being interrogated even in the most civil way about her performance right after a game is not only counterproductive, it can start building a psychological wall between you and your child. If the youngster begins to think that she is going to be quizzed and graded after every game, before too long your child is going to turn off from playing that sport—not necessarily because she doesn't enjoy it, but because she knows she's going to have to sit through a stringent performance evaluation from Mom or Dad after each game.

Sure, this sounds like the script from the old baseball movie "Fear Strikes Out." But while most parents would say that the Jimmy Piersall story—the basis for this film—was overly dramatized, the fact remains that too many parents fall into the same behavior pattern.

Some Rules to Remember
Especially when your kids are young (ages six through twelve), it's up to you to play the role of "mature adult" and not fall into the role of "critical parent."

By that I mean you're going to have to do things and say things that are appropriate for your child. Here are a few simple rules to remember when the game is over and you're all piling into the family station wagon:

* Let your child enjoy the experience of having played the game.

  Make sure that she had fun. If not, find out why . Let her talk. Let her tell you what wasn't fun, and take her feelings seriously. Maybe she got into a fight with one of her teammates. Or maybe the coach said something to her that hurt her feelings. Whatever the problem is, listen to the details and let your child talk.

  If it turns out to be something you can address or deal with, then do so. Again, the first rule of youth sports is for you, to get involved. So do it.

* Right after the game don't offer any criticism—even of the so-called "constructive" kind.

I call this "the station wagon syndrome." Well-meaning parents get their young athlete in the family station, and before they have even left the field's parking lot, they are already offering a critique of the kid's performance. Remember this one rule: right after a game, all an athlete wants to hear is praise. Praise for her efforts. Sincere praise.

If you feel compelled to discuss the game with your child, wait several hours. Perhaps after dinner or before they go to bed. By then the game will be easier to talk about—both from the child's point of view and your own. Just remember not to force the conversation on your child.

- Ask them what part of the game they enjoyed the most.

That's a good question to ask. Let the child retell his version of the game. What was most fun for him might surprise you.

Example: I remember when my six-year-old scored a terrific goal in a soccer game. Afterward I asked which part of the game was the most fun. Naturally, I figured he would talk about the goal being scored since he'd kicked the ball into the net. But to my surprise he was much prouder of a ball he had kicked earlier in the game when he had sort of "punted" the ball high in the air. To him that play was a lot more spectacular—and more fun—than scoring a goal.

Anytime you can get your child to talk about the game with great verve and enthusiasm that's a solid sign that the experience was a positive one for him.

- Make the game a fun experience for everyone.

Make it a part of your "game-day ritual" to stop afterward for ice cream or soda or pizza. But one very important point: Make certain that you stop after the game on losing days as well as winning ones!

What If Your Child Is Upset with Her Performance?

Let's face it. Kids are smarter than we give them credit for, and they're often aware of their performance. If they strike out in a big situation, let the winning goal go by, or make a mistake in a gymnastics performance, they become disappointed and angry with themselves.

As a parent when you see your child struggle in situations like this, your first reaction is somehow to reach out and reassure her. That's fine. But as you console your child, remember that you shouldn't downplay the incident either. Too often a parent will say to the child who has struggled, "That's okay honey, the game isn't that big a deal...."

Certainly, your heart is in the right place. After all, by attempting to keep the game in perspective, you're trying to minimize your child's sense of personal failure. But remember that from the child's point of view that game was a big deal—at least in her young life. Thus, your compassionate attempt to downplay that game only adds more misery and frustration to the child's perception.

After a tough game or event in which your child has not played well—and she knows it—give her the breathing room to experience that sense of frustration. You can hug her, applaud her on her bright moments, and try to keep the conversation on an even keel. But if your child is sad because of the game, don't dismiss the event as being meaningless. Rather, give your child some time to feel it, absorb it, and then after a while, get her attention focused on the day's next activity.

Later that night during a quiet time you can talk about the moments of frustration from that day's game or event. In other words, learning how to cope with losing is just as important for a child as learning how to cope with winning.

1. Associated Press wire story, June 23, 1991.
2. *The New York Times*, July 24, 1988.
3. *The Hartford Courant*, February 19, 1991.
4. *Rockland Journal-News* (White Plains, N.Y.), June 16, 1991.
5. *Sport magazine*, September 1989, p. 65.
6. *Newsweek*, May 27, 1989.

CHAPTER 4

Your Position: The Parent

Being the parent of a child playing in an organized youth sports league is, for most people, a fairly substantial commitment. During the course of any sports season, all sorts of team developments, confrontations, conflicts, and problems are going to crop up.

Throughout the remainder of this book, I shall attempt to deal with as many situations as I can that may occur in youth sports. But the following developments are so common for many parents and their children that I thought we'd deal with them right now—just to get the ball rolling.

Case #1: You tell your child to get dressed and ready for the youth league game and she simply says, "I don't want to go today. I want to stay here and watch television."

Case #2: Your child realizes that his team is about to lose a game. When the game does come to an end, your child runs to you with tears streaming down his face.

Case #3: You're watching your child play in a youth league game when a kid from the other team throws a punch at your child for seemingly no reason at all.

Case #4: Your child enjoys being on the team, but he also happens to be the youngest—and the least talented. As the season goes by, he plays less and less. You don't know whether you should talk to the coach. And if you do, what would you say and how would you say it?

Case #5: Your child happens to be the oldest—and the most talented—player on the team. As a result, she scores all the goals, dominates the play of the game, and as the season goes on begins to show off a bit too much in front of the other players. What, if anything, should you say to your daughter and what should you say to the coach?

Case #6: In the course of a game, there is a minor collision between your son and another kid from the opposing team. Concerned about your boy's health and welfare, you run onto the field to see if he's okay. He says he's all right and wants to keep playing. You look at him and think he ought to come out. What do you do?

Case #7: You're watching your child play in a game, and the coach from the opposing team is loud and screaming all sorts of obscenities. Your team has never heard such awful things before. After a while it becomes apparent that the other coach is not going to stop and that his behavior has become downright embarrassing. Do you simply ask the opposing coach to stop? Do you protest to the official/umpire? Or do you pull your kids off the playing field?

Finding the Mature Adult in You

If you have a child playing organized youth sports, chances are you've experienced any number of the above scenarios. The problem is, there are really no simple solutions to these common dilemmas. Nevertheless, as a mature adult you have to take certain actions on each one, however unpopular or unpleasant.

The point has been made before, but it bears repeating: As a parent who is overseeing this kind of youth league competition it's incumbent upon you and your peers to ensure that all of the sports activity is conducted in an intelligent, mature manner. In other words, somebody has to act like an adult out there so it might as well be you.

Don't worry—there will be plenty of other parents whose behavior will be just as puerile and prepubescent as the behavior of your kids. You have to watch out for these boorish parents and make certain that their behavior doesn't ruin the fun of others or, for that matter, simply set a poor example for the kids.

Case #1: The Reluctant Athlete

Suppose your child tells you that she doesn't want to get dressed for the game this afternoon and would prefer to stay home.

Should you be concerned? Should you let her have her way? What about a sense of commitment to the team and to the other players?

All good questions. But before you start figuring out what your approach should be and how you're going to talk with your child, the first thing you ought to find out is why she doesn't want to go. Keep in mind that this kind of thing does happen occasionally, and it's essential that you don't blow it out of proportion.

Rather than take a hard line about your child's obligation to play ("You signed up for the team, so you had better play or else!"), try a softer, more mature approach. Sit down with your child and try to find out why she doesn't want to go. After all, if she really did want to play, you wouldn't have this kind of situation on your hands. Your best bet is to talk with her and try to discover what the underlying problem is.

Sometimes it's because the child doesn't think she is good enough or as talented as the other players. Or it might be because the coach raised his voice to her last week and that memory is still troubling her. Or maybe it's because one of her teammates was mean to her last week or somebody poked fun at her or teased her. Maybe she's afraid of getting hurt. And sometimes it's nothing more than the child's feeling poorly and not wanting to play.

The point is, let children tell you what's wrong. Don't allow them to become defensive or to simply say that "nothing's wrong." Let them know that they don't have to play if they really don't want to, but that they have to have a reason why they don't want to play. Again, let them talk but don't let them off the hook.

More times than not they will come up with the truth. Be prepared to handle some tears at this juncture because most children do enjoy and look forward to playing. But if there's a conflict that the child wants to avoid, she is going to be torn between wanting to play and having to confront an unruly coach, a mean teammate, or some other fear. Once the problem is brought out, you can begin to address it properly.

But What about Commitment?
No question that teaching a child a sense of obligation and commitment is one of the key lessons of playing on a youth team. That's something that should be reinforced at various times of the year, as in "You know, Mary/Michael, when you sign up for a team, it's your responsibility to attend all the practice sessions and be on time for the games. If you don't believe you can do that, then we ought to think again about your commitment before we sign up. After all, playing for a team means being somebody who can be counted on."

With most youth teams the rules of obligation are usually quite simple: If you don't come to practice on time and work hard, don't expect to play a lot in the game that week. For most kids that's a pretty standard rule. It's easy to accept and easy to follow.

But there are going to be times in the course of a season when a child will have to miss a practice or game; family obligations, vacations, and sickness can get in the way. As a parent you share the responsibility with your child to let the team's coach know just as soon as possible when these conflicts are going to come up.

But make it a point to have your child—not you—call the coach to tell her that he can't make it that week to practice or a game. Let your child—not you—explain why he can't make it. Only in the case of illness should the child not have to make the call.

Such a practice reinforces a sense of responsibility and commitment, as well as an understanding of how important it is to communicate with other adults. This interaction may sound incredibly simple, but you'd be surprised at how many major league athletes in this day and age have never learned how to take on responsibility. Somebody has always been there to make those calls for them. As you can imagine, this can lead to all sorts of problems when these pro athletes finish playing and have to readjust to the "real world."

Commitment, then, is an important concept for your child to come to grips with, but always let your child have the first opportunity to explain why he doesn't want to play. More often than not, underlying reasons are quickly brought forth. And once the problem is out on the table, it's easier to deal with.

Question: What about the Star Who Always Shows Up Late?

Every team seems to have one: the star player who takes advantage of his abilities and tends to show up late for practices (or misses practice entirely without any reason) but is always on time for the start of the game.

Now, some coaches see this as a difficult dilemma. "After all," the coach rationalizes, "if I penalize my star player for missing practice and force him to sit out a large portion of the game, then I'm not just punishing him—I'm punishing the rest of the team!" Such a philosophy seems to suggest that winning in the youth leagues is always the top priority.

Well, maybe that's a tough judgment call if you're coaching in the NFL or in the NBA. But at the youth sports level, however, not only is it your obligation to bench that star player, but if you don't, you're only going to ruin his sense of responsibility and team commitment. If the kid never learns about being on time and attending practice sessions when he's ten or eleven, by the time he reaches high school, he'll be totally out of control and impossible to discipline. Why? Because nobody had the guts to lay down the law to him when he was younger.

Here's an easy answer: If the star player doesn't understand about being on time and doesn't respect team obligations, make certain that his parents understand the rules. If he persists in being late or being unruly in practice, then he doesn't play much. Period.

Eventually, if that star player really wants to play, he'll get the message: Come to practice and be on time.

Case #2: The Tearful Loser
The most important—but tricky—lesson you can teach your child about losing is that it happens, that it's okay, and that he'll get over it.

On the other hand, everybody wants to be a winner, and you obviously want your child to win a lot more often than he loses. Let's face it—winning is a lot more fun than losing.

But the point here is a simple one: Don't overreact. Let your child have a few tears. He's disappointed. He wanted to win. He tried hard. And yet, he lost. Just because parents don't often react to losing a game with tears doesn't mean that a child can't.

And by the way, it makes no difference how old the child is. He can be six, ten, sixteen, or older. You've seen top college athletes lose themselves in their tears after a big loss so why can't kids?

Whatever you do, don't make a big deal out of it and don't try to make your child stop it or become a "macho" kind of person who keeps his emotions within. Remember that crying and tears are basic, essential human expressions just like laughter and smiling, and they should not be repressed. You wouldn't tell your child not to laugh or smile; don't tell him not to cry if he feels bad.

"Yes—I understand what you're saying, but what about the kid who cries almost all the time?"

It might be a little embarrassing right now for you, as the parent, to have to put up with a child who greets all setbacks, both major and minor, with tears. But don't worry. He'll grow out of it. Don't punish the child or belittle him because of his tears. That will do nothing except add to his misery and lower his self-esteem.

Sooner or later peer pressure enters into the picture; kids suddenly don't like to have their classmates or teammates see them cry. It may take a little while for this peer-pressure process to set in, but don't worry— it will. And the tears will begin to dry up quickly.

Case #3: When It Comes to Fighting, "Kids Will Be Kids"

Nonsense. If you see your kid, or any other kid, throw a punch or try intentionally to injure another player, be a mature adult, step in, and stop it immediately. Don't complain to the ref. Don't complain to the coach. You take charge. Get involved right now—even if it means stopping the game—and separate the puncher from the punchee.

You might have noticed that in the professional ranks of sports, there is no place for fighting, and that athletes who can't keep their emotions in check and follow the no-fighting rule are usually thrown out of the game. That's a good rule at the professional level and an even better rule at the youth league level. Enforce it.

"But what happens if it's my child who's an innocent victim, and he didn't throw any punches?"

Before punitive action is taken, get both sides of the story from each kid as best you can. If it turns out that both sides were at fault, let them both sit out.

But sometimes you'll run into kids who just don't know how to behave themselves. In the heat of action, they'll lash out and punch an unsuspecting player. When this happens, it's up to you to inform the ref and the player's coach of what happened, and let them take punitive action. Usually, that means having the miscreant child sit out for the rest of the game, or at least for several minutes or innings.

Again, the point is, as a mature adult and parent, you can't condone any violent action, whether it's deliberate or nondeliberate. It has to be addressed and dealt with right away.

Case #4: "My Kid Is a Daisy-Picker"

Parents like to gauge their kids as athletes and compare their athletic abilities to those of the other kids in the class. But how silly! When your kids are six or eight or ten, don't worry so much about whether they're the best athletes in the school. Focus more on whether they're enjoying the experience.

Why? Because if they enjoy playing that particular sport, your kids will be more eager than ever to spend time practicing and developing their skills as they get older. Remember—the self-motivated child is the one who will always end up being among the best.

"But the coach wants to win, and he always puts my child in right field and bats him ninth...."

Okay, the coach may not be as patient as you are. But if you're concerned that your child is being shunted off to the side, there's no reason why you can't talk to the coach about the problem. Before you do, however, here are a couple of ideas.

One, don't talk to the coach about the problem right before or during the game. First of all, that's not fair to the coach, who has to shepherd not just your child but all the rest of the kids. Besides, you don't want the other parents to think that you're trying to curry special favors from the coach. Instead, try the telephone. The conversation between you and the coach will be private, and you'll have time to get your points across in a civil and relaxed manner. The same goes for the coach.

Two, have the courage to realize that your child may not be the most gifted athlete around—at least at his present age. This realization allows the coach a little breathing room. After all, you can certainly get the point across that you'd like to have your child get a little more quality playing time, but you also recognize that your child may not be the best.

Rather than demanding that your child get more of an opportunity, talk with the coach to see if a compromise can be worked out. You'll find that more times than not, a coach will be much more responsive to your child's needs with this kind of approach than with a confrontational one.

Case #5: "My Kid Is the Star...."
Sometimes it's just as difficult to be the parent of one of the more talented players. By the time kids are eight- or nine-years-old, they begin to sense who the best players are. This is not a bad thing; rather, it's to be expected as part of their natural evolution in competitive sports.

Being considered a good athlete by one's peers usually brings only good things to one's self-esteem. But, as with so many things in life, too much of a good thing can sometimes lead to trouble. If your child is one of those gifted athletes, that's great—so long as she keeps her sense of fair play in balance.

Basically, when it comes to performing on the field, whether your child is the least or the most talented, the rules of sportsmanship apply to all players in the same democratic way. This means that losers shouldn't whine and winners shouldn't show off. And it's up to the parents to supervise and scrutinize these behaviors.

On an individual basis, if your child seems to be losing her sense of sportsmanship, then lay the law down right away. Start by first addressing the question of her behavior on a one-to-one basis. Off the field, either before or after the game, explain to your child that showing off is not only bad sportsmanship, but serves no constructive purpose. All it does is get other people upset and angry with her. It takes away from the admiration that other kids and parents have for her athletic talents.

If that doesn't get through, then try a "tough love" approach. Instruct the coach or coaches to remove your child from the game whenever this obnoxious behavior is manifested. This approach almost always works, because if there is one thing a talented kid wants to do, it's play in the game. And if she is penalized for her behavior and not allowed to play, eventually she'll get the message that showing off is simply not acceptable on the field.

"But what if the coach doesn't take my child out of the game?" Good question, but again, explain to the coach that you really don't want to tolerate this kind of obnoxious behavior and that following your repeated warnings to the child, she has now been told that if she doesn't clean up her act, she'll be benched. It's up to the coach to respect your wishes. After all, you're trying to teach the child a lesson in civility; it's up to the coach to enforce it.

Above all, this is the kind of behavior that should be addressed as soon as it is witnessed. Don't let it grow. Nip it in the bud at an early age.

Case #6: What about Injuries on the Field?
There's nothing more frightening for a parent than to see one's child get hurt during the course of a game. Most parents react instinctively and want to run out on the field to see if their little one is okay.

For the most part I encourage this, particularly at the younger ages, from five or six right up to ten. For most children in that age bracket, getting hurt on an athletic field is a relatively new experience and they are so stunned and shocked that they tend to overreact and burst into tears right away. Even when the hurt is relatively minor, the child still tends to turn to tears simply as a reflexive defense mechanism.

In most cases I prefer that the game be stopped and the parent and/or coach be allowed to check on the child. If he wishes, the child can come off the field for a few minutes. Once he has regained his composure and is certain that the hurt was only momentary, he should be allowed back into the game right away.

This kind of experience allows the child to deal with pain, to overcome it, and then to let his enthusiasm for the game overcome his fears of getting hurt again. And the parent comes away relieved that their child wasn't hurt seriously and still wants to play.

Obviously, if there is any suspicion that the child is hurt somewhat seriously, then no chances should be taken at all. Especially with any kind of head injury or collision, the child ought to be checked out thoroughly, if need be by a doctor at the nearest hospital. No game—especially at this age—is important enough to risk your child's health. Don't take the chance by sending him back to play when he might be seriously injured.

Case #7: The Obscene Opposing Coach

Let's take the situation of an opposing coach who likes to mix in plenty of vulgarities and obscenities when coaching the kids. (I say *opposing* coach here, because certainly the coach of your children's team would never swear, right?) You as a parent can take one of two approaches.

You can simply ignore what's going on and tell your children to "close their ears" and ignore the other coach; a relatively simple but hardly satisfactory way out of the problem. Quite frankly, it just doesn't work.

Choice number two is a little more difficult. First, I would go to the referee/umpire/official and point out that the opposing coach is not only violating the spirit of the league (all youth leagues of all ages eschew the use of obscenities), but that he is simply making things quite difficult for you and the other parents.

Usually, the official will make a point then and there of saying something to the other coach. And often the coach is so embarrassed at being singled out for this kind of behavior that he will shut up right away.

But sometimes the official will listen to your complaint, simply shrug his shoulders, and say "What can I do? If the guy wants to cuss, I really can't stop him." This happens often when the ref/ump/official is just a teenager who is working the game. After all, how many 18 year olds are going to tell a grown-up coach with a foul mouth to knock it off?

And then there are those occasions where the opposing coach is warned by the ref, blows him off, and says, "I can say anything I want when I'm coaching. And besides, my kids know that when I swear, I don't mean anything by it."

In the best of all worlds, a simple complaint to the ref would have solved the problem. But when the ref is too young or too intimidated to say anything, or when the opposing coach doesn't want to hear about it, it's time for the mature adult in you to take a stand.

The best choice is simply to go over to your team's coach and insist that the game be stopped until the opposing coach cleans up his act. By now the other parents on your side of the field will have noticed the unruly behavior, and they should support you in your actions. Tell the coach that either the game comes to a stop, or you're taking your child off the field and will complain directly to the league's supervising board. But make certain you have the guts to follow through!

Being a Good Parent Is Difficult

If you haven't noticed by now—and I'm sure you have—then understand that being a good parent to a growing athlete can be a difficult proposition. And that role is never more complex than when you let your child play for someone other than yourself.

All of us want only the best for our children, but when you let them play for another parent, you're asking a lot of yourself. Questions like: Can I keep my own emotions in check? Can I walk the sidelines and watch my child without interfering? Can I exhibit the kind of positive behavior that will make my child's experience a good one?

Beyond that, when your child goes out on the field of athletic competition, do you trust her? Trust her in the sense that she can now make her own decisions, knows what kind of behavior is acceptable, and knows how to respect the word of her coaches and referees? This can and should be a wonderful time for your child and for you and your family. Ultimately, it all comes down to trust. Along those lines, keep the words on the following page with you:

There are little eyes upon you,
And they're watching night and day;
There are little ears that quickly
Take in every word you say;
There are little hands all eager
To do anything you do;
And a little boy who's dreaming
Of the day he'll be like you.

You're the little fellow's idol;
You're the wisest of the wise,
In his little mind about you,
No suspicions ever rise;
He believes in you devoutly,
Holds that all you can say and do,
He will say and do, in your way
When he's a grown-up like you.

There's a wide-eyed little fellow
Who believes you're always right,
And his ears are always open,
And he watches day and night;
You are setting an example
Every day in all you do,
For the little boy who's waiting
To grow up to be like you.

—Author unknown

CHAPTER 5

The Coach

Tom Grieve and his family live in Arlington, Texas. Like so many parents, he had a busy career that tended to keep him on the road a lot during the spring and summer.

But as his children began to grow up, Tom realized that although he loved his career, he loved his family even more. Consequently, he became interested in his kids' involvement in youth sports leagues, particularly Little League baseball. "I wasn't so concerned with my boys, Tim and Ben, learning the finer points of the game," says Grieve. "I was more concerned that they played for coaches who made the experience a positive, supportive one—one that was fun for the kids."

In the early years Grieve was generally happy with the coaches that his kids played for. But more recently he's been less than thrilled with the coaching environment. "It got to the point where I had to make a decision, and even though my job tends to keep me in the office late into the night, I realized that I'd rather spend my time with my kids, sharing their ball-playing experience." As a result, Grieve first became an assistant coach and then ultimately a head coach for his kids' Little League teams.

For Grieve this dedication to coaching Little League was a major decision. After all, during this time he was also the general manager of the Texas Rangers baseball team. Spending time with his boys and coaching them in the spring and summer, meant time spent away from the Rangers' major league club. Reflects Grieve: "I remember Frank Lucchesi, a longtime major league manager, used to tell me that kids grow up fast, and that whatever I do, to make certain I found time for them. Because once they're gone, they're gone. I've always remembered that advice, and I try to live by it. Especially as it applies to Little League."

Like other parents, Grieve has seen his share of unnecessary pressures placed on kids playing ball. "I can't ever remember going to a game in which I didn't hear some parent or coach yelling and screaming at one of their kids or players. And these are intelligent, educated people! But just last night I was at a game and the third-base coach was yelling at his son, who was batting at the time, 'When are you going to swing at a pitch that you can handle? What's wrong with you? Don't you want to get better?' I hear that kind of stuff all the time. And it drives me nuts."

What It Means to Be a Coach

Tom Grieve's decision to become more personally involved in his kids' Little League activities is not uncommon. In fact, it is a rule in most organized youth sports leagues that a parent must involve herself to some extent with her child's team. That can take the form of bringing refreshments to the games, helping umpire or referee a game, or in many cases, serving as either the head or assistant coach.

But for some reason too many parents look upon coaching duty as a dreaded chore. And that's a real shame because serving as a coach on your child's team is a terrific way to strengthen the lines of communication between you and your child. Why? Because there are few opportunities in your child's life and your own in which you are both working (and playing) together toward a common goal. If nothing else, getting to know your child and his/her teammates can serve as a real window of observation through which to see how your child reacts to teammates, competition, and organized play.

Here are a few of the common excuses parents use to beg off having to coach:

- "I really don't know much about the sport and would feel unprepared trying to explain it."

- "I'm just too busy with work and other obligations to get involved with coaching kids."

- "I lose my temper too easily with youngsters. I just wouldn't be good at it."

There are literally hundreds of excuses. But if you're an uninvolved parent, don't expect too much from your child in terms of sharing a common experience. Simply going to the game on Saturday or Sunday isn't enough if you want your child to learn to enjoy and understand the parameters of the particular team sport he or she is playing.

But let's assume you are involved, that you've signed up as a head coach or an assistant coach. The next question is "Now what do I do?"

Start at the Beginning

Let's assume further that you don't know squat about the sport. Don't know a baseball from a hockey puck. That's okay, but it also means you've got to stay a few steps ahead of the kids. First thing, get yourself to your town's public library. Take out a few books on the basics of the sport your child is playing—and read them!

Most leagues usually hand out some sort of coaching literature. But be forewarned. Many of these coaching books assume you already know all the rules of the sport. Worse, many of them are so poorly written that the most basic questions about the sport are not covered (how many players on a team, what happens in case of a tie, and so on).

Take the most basic books you can find in the library on that particular sport and read through these books together, just as you would read any book to your child in the evening. You can learn about the sport together, and along the way it will be doubly educational for parent and child.

From there you should get in the habit of actually practicing some of the skills you've read about with your son or daughter. This doesn't have to take much time, but any time you spend playing with your kids is well worth the effort. Besides, it'll be fun.

Let's assume that your six-year-old daughter has signed up for a soccer league. Now, most six-year-olds have very little understanding about the rules of soccer, except for the fact that you aren't allowed to touch the ball with your hands (unless you're the goalie). That's fine. Spend some time with her trying to develop her sense of kicking a ball, first with her right foot and then, if she wants to try it, with her left.

Although this kind of basic kicking skill may seem awfully simple to you, for most children it takes some time and effort. It may even be frustrating for her at the beginning, but stay with it and offer all the positive encouragement and enthusiasm you can muster. Reward each of her attempts with great praise; don't worry about the actual result. It's the effort you're trying to applaud, not the actual kick.

Time should be a concern here. On the one hand, you don't want to brush your child off with just a few seconds of effort. On the other hand, if you find yourself spending more than twenty minutes on this drill, you might want to consider backing off. Twenty minutes is awfully long for a child's attention span. By the end of that time, she might be beginning to turn away from your tutelage.

And speaking of coaching, use some common sense here. Remember that a six-year-old can handle only so much instruction. The same goes for an eight-year-old, ten-year-old, twelve-year-old, and up. Gauge how much personalized and detailed coaching you give your child based upon her age and interest in what you have to say.

Finally, don't make the mistake of competing with your child. That may sound silly, but lots of parents will actually let their child practice a new skill for a while, and then the parent will say, "Okay, let's see who does it better" or "Let's see if you can stop my shot."

There's no need for this. Even though a parent will say, "I was just fooling around," the child doesn't see it that way. Your son or daughter sees you as another competitor or opponent, except for the fact that you'll probably beat him or her in any sporting endeavor. It may start out as a sporting challenge for your child, but it will quickly dissolve into frustration. Just be aware of the hazards of this kind of challenge.

> What do you do with the youngster who always wants to do certain skills his own way and won't listen to coaching?

This happens all the time, especially among the more talented kids. Because a youngster may already have developed some skills on his own, he may be quite reluctant to listen to you/the parent/the coach try to tell him how to change his approach. After all, he's quite proud of his mastered skills; to have to learn a new method would mean more work and more effort for him, not to mention a blow to his self-esteem.

So, rather than get into a shouting match with your child, simply ask him to sit for a few minutes to watch how you would practice a certain skill, such as throwing a baseball or dribbling a soccer ball. You don't have to draw any comparisons, or for that matter make any comment. You might add, "This is the way I learned how to dribble a soccer ball—now show me how you learned to do it."

Don't make the mistake of saying, "My way is the better way," or "Why don't you at least try it my way?" or "This is how the major leaguers do it." If your child is sharp and somewhat observant, while he may be reluctant in your presence to try your style or approach, chances are that when he gets out on the playground with no parents or coaches around, he will secretly try it your way. Then, before long he too will realize why your way is better and will adopt it as his own.

Are kids that smart? Sure they are. In fact, many of them grow up to be parents themselves.

Use Positive Feedback As a Motivator

If there is one simple rule that every youth league coach should understand, it's that all children respond to positive feedback and encouragement. No volume of yelling or screaming you do is ever going to have as much long-term impact as a few kind, sincere words of praise.

And there's an even better side-effect of praising young players: The more they know that you, as their coach, feel good about their efforts, the better they feel about themselves.

You've heard all those maxims about sports building a strong sense of character? Well, that's where a strong sense of character comes from—from the coach who goes out of his or her way to make certain every player is praised.

Let's put it another way, on a more adult level. Suppose you had your choice of two bosses to work for. Boss Number One tells you how good you could be if only you worked harder and longer than your competitors. While he's a nice enough guy most of the time, during the crunch times he becomes a real bear, yelling and screaming at you to work harder.

Boss Number Two also tells you how good you could be if you worked hard. But rather than yelling at you, he spends most of his time trying to praise and motivate you, complimenting you when you do good work. He always seems to keep an even disposition, even under the toughest pressure.

Question: Which boss would you rather work for? Second question: Which company would you feel more motivated to work for?

Most likely you're going to select Boss Number Two. Not surprisingly, kids would respond in the same way if, instead of a boss, we were talking about a coach and the youngster's team.

The point is, all people—kids included—respond in a better, more motivated fashion when the authority figure they report to uses praise as a motivational force, not threats or sarcasm.

Build Them Up

If there's one similarity between being a parent off the field and being a coach on the field, it's this simple rule: When it comes to maintaining your child's self-esteem, always remember to praise (or criticize) his or her behavior—don't criticize him or her as a person.

Example: A seven-year-old soccer player accustomed to playing goalie has been moved to fullback. During the course of a 1-1 game, the ball comes to the child and out of instinct from playing goalie, he reaches down and grabs the ball with both hands, which is, of course, against the rules.

The whistle blows, and the other team is awarded a penalty kick. One of the players kicks the ball hard, and it goes into the net.

The seven-year-old who grabbed the ball by accident is old enough to grasp the reality of the situation. If he had merely kicked the ball instead of using his hands, the other team wouldn't have had a penalty kick and been able to score the goal.

The critical moment has arrived for his team's coach. Let's say he gathers his team together and says to the seven-year-old something like "My gosh Adam, what's wrong with you? You knew you weren't playing goalie anymore didn't you? C'mon. Sometimes I just wonder where your head is at!"

A tongue-lashing like that might be justified if the coach were working with a group of pro soccer players. But with seven-year-olds, the coach has merely accomplished one point: He has made that seven-year-old feel like he's totally worthless. True, the lesson will stay with him; for the rest of his life, that little boy will always remember that incredibly embarrassing moment and how it was further burned into a humiliating memory by his coach.

All things considered, it's not the kind of experience you want for your child.

On the other hand, suppose the coach had the proper perspective on this. Sure, she wants the kids to win and do well on the soccer field. But on the other hand, the more enlightened coach is going to gather the team together and talk about the team's general behavior and not make personal comments. Something like "Okay, kids, I think we can all learn something from Adam's touching the ball out there. We all know, don't we, that only the goalie is allowed to use his hands, right? Now, the next time you're tempted to pick up a ball during a game, just ask yourself first whether you're the goalie. Okay, any questions? Let's get back and score a goal."

Remember, the child is well aware that he cost his team a goal, so there's no reason to reemphasize that reality. It's up to the coach then to be constructive in her approach and not let that bad moment linger either in Adam's mind or with the rest of the team.

Again, *never* focus your remarks on the child's *personality*. You can remark on his behavior—but not on whether he's a good or bad kid.

How important is self-esteem? Well, it's been proven time and again that people who develop strong self-esteem also develop a strong self-confidence in their abilities, are able to interact with others well, and understand social accountability and responsibility. Those who don't develop a solid sense of self-esteem often have bouts with depression, have difficulty in relating to others, tend to be overly jealous, and are more tempted to look for solace in substance abuse.

Youth sports leagues are, among other things, set up with the purpose of increasing or enhancing a child's developing sense of self-esteem. But it's not often easy to do that, especially in competitive situations. Above all, be careful not to push a child too strongly or to try to measure him against his peers. Says Dr. Marvin I. Gottlieb, Director of the Institute for Child Development at the Hackensack Medical Center in New Jersey: "Not every child has the same timetable for development, and they all don't react the same way."[1]

If there's one overriding lesson that too many youth coaches forget, it's the impact that their negative words and comments have on young kids. Nothing can do more to hurt a child's self-esteem than a few caustic or sarcastic comments made by a coach spoken in a moment of uncontrolled anger or disappointment.

Motivation and Team Play

Successful coaches in any sport and at any level will tell you that the secret of success is not to make the players adapt to his or her style, but rather for the coach to adapt to the players.

The youth league coach can have her own basic ideas about coaching, but must always seek to know her players and their distinctive personalities. Being a strict disciplinarian is just not going to work with teams full of seven- and eight-year-olds. By the same token, ten- and eleven-year-olds are not going to respond to a coach who is disorganized or who doesn't take the games or practices seriously.

During the early season practices, get to know your players. The best coaches make a habit of this, and they do it simply by walking around the field and spending a little time with each player. Talk to them. Get them to smile and laugh. Let them know that you are somebody who can be trusted and looked up to, somebody they can always approach with a thought, comment, or worry.

Then there's the other kind of approach—the so called aloof coach who simply barks out orders, tells the kids to do certain drills, and then simply watches from the side, not really getting personally involved. Invariably, these coaches run their teams like little military units, and while they may sometimes be successful, the overall learning experience is a negative one for the children.

The Types of Youth Coaches

As you might imagine, youth league coaches can fall into various classifications. Listed below are some stereotypes that, ideally, you do not resemble. But if you find any of these coaching styles sounding like you (or like your child's coach), then take care and take appropriate action.

The Drill Sergeant

He is the one alluded to above who runs practices and games with a strict, no-nonsense approach. His philosophy is summed up in the phrase, "The only way to have fun in sports is to win—and win all the time."

As discussed earlier, kids normally take their sporting endeavors very seriously. For them, "playing" sports is serious work. That's okay when you're a kid. But when the coach, who's presumably an adult, takes winning and losing just as seriously, and maybe even more so, than the kids, you're looking at problems.

If your child happens to end up on a team like this, you ought seriously to consider getting him moved to another team right away. Because he'll play the entire season out of a fear of losing rather than for the joy of playing.

The Screaming Apologist

A close cousin to the Drill Sergeant is the coach who takes winning very seriously, and who acknowledges before each game that "while I may occasionally raise my voice during the course of the game, please understand that I'm just yelling because of all the excitement and simply because I want you all to play so well."

You know the routine. This sweet-sounding apologist then goes out and hoots and hollers at every kid during the action. By the end of the game, the coach (especially if the team has won) is all smiles and sweetness again. Meanwhile the kids have started to flinch at the idea of playing in a game in front of this kind of maniac.

If you find your child playing for such a coach, you should first give him the benefit of the doubt and explain that you were a bit concerned about the amount of yelling that took place during the game. Warning: If the coach just brushes you off with a casual "Oh yeah, I know—I'm real loud, aren't I?" and laughs , then you know you've got problems. But if the coach says, "Gee, I had no idea how loud I was," then you can at least monitor the coach and point out his behavior to him when he gets loud again.

As with any team or coach, it's up to you, the parent/adult, to observe and, if necessary, get involved.

The Major League Know-It-All

It's rare to see a professional athlete try to work with kids and change the way a child does something, whether it be the way the child swings a bat, shoots a basketball, or kicks a soccer ball.

Professional athletes—people who make their living playing sports—usually know all too well that there are many, many ways to perform a particular skill in sports. Just look, for example, at how many different styles of major league hitters there are—some batters choke up, some take long, looping swings, some punch at the ball.

The point is, pro athletes know and fully understand that there are many ways to skin a sporting cat.

But now, check out any youth sports league. Chances are good that on any given weekend you'll find a coach who is busy changing every kid's style to conform to what he thinks is best. "Hold the bat this way!" is a typical refrain. Before too long all the kids on the team—no matter their size, weight, strength, or ability—are holding the bat in the same fashion. And they do it because the coach insists they do it his way.

It makes no difference whether the coach's system is good, bad, or indifferent—let the child experiment and find her own style of play. Coaches can start getting involved and tinkering with the child's form when the child is in junior high or high school, but in the youth leagues let her do it the way she enjoys and feels comfortable with.

Remember the story of Steve Olin, the sidearm pitcher in the big leagues? He had thrown the ball in that peculiar, unorthodox fashion from the time he was in Little League, but every coach he had had tried to change his style and insisted that he throw the ball overhand. Credit Olin's stubbornness in sticking to his sidearm delivery, because the way Steve tells it, if he had changed to overhand he would never have gotten a pro contract, much less a chance at the major leagues.

The Casual Coach

At the other extreme is the casual coach who takes things, well, a little too casually. She is the one who shows up for practice without ever giving the practice session or the game a moment's notice beforehand.

While kids certainly will fill in this kind of void with their own pickup games, this totally disorganized approach actually gets in the way of the children's learning from the experience of youth sports. It's up to the coach to teach and instruct and to give the children an idea of organization and a semblance of structure. You can allow the children to have fun and enjoy the games, but especially as the kids reach the age of ten, they expect you as a coach to offer them a feel for a game plan, a sense of purpose, and a feeling of teamsmanship.

The disorganized coach who comes to the practices and games with papers flying in different directions, not enough or the wrong equipment, or with no sense of what is going to happen that day turns a potentially wonderful sporting event into a potential disaster by his disregard for the responsibility of the job.

If your child plays for a coach like this, there's only one tactic to follow—get more involved. Take the coach to the side and volunteer your services immediately. Don't worry about your lack of knowledge of the game; remember, you're not coaching the San Francisco 49ers or the New York Mets here. Rather, if you simply add a solid dose of organization and a sense of discipline when it comes to being on time for practices and for the game, your presence will do wonders—both for the team and for the head coach.

The Conniver

Every league, sadly, has a coach like this. He is the one who is already checking for every loophole, or every competitive angle, and is determined to make certain his team is amply loaded with more than its share of the most talented kids in the league.

The conniving coach can work his magic in several ways. Some make certain that they are on the roster committees—the league governing body that determines which teams in the league get which players. In this somewhat subversive manner, the conniving coach can personally oversee which players end up on his roster.

This becomes a particularly difficult situation if the rest of the coaches in the league aren't as concerned with winning at all costs as the conniver is. When the teams have been formed and the conniver has succeeded in stacking together the team he wants, most of the other coaches can do nothing more than shrug their shoulders in disgust. It's almost as though the other coaches/parents are admitting, "Yeah, we now realize that he/she stacked the team roster with the best players, but what can we do now?"

Plenty. Make a serious and concerted appeal to the league's commissioner to balance the teams in the league. And if the commissioner won't hear of such a move ("After all, we're already well into the season . . .") or if the commissioner just happens to be one of the best friends of the conniving coach, you can file a formal protest with the league's national governing body. Or if you feel strongly enough, withdraw your team from league competition and encourage other teams to follow suit.

The point is, by simply shrugging your shoulders, you are quietly accepting and condoning what the conniving coach has done. Remember—the kids themselves won't be fooled. They know who the better players are and you'll have a difficult time trying to explain why one team seems to have more of the better or older players than the other teams do.

The "Professional"

This is the coach who can't do enough to prepare her team. Scouting reports on each opposing team. Injury updates. Field conditions. The latest weather forecast. The latest gimmicks in motivation to keep her players ready to perform. Guest speakers who motivate. Weekly newsletters. And of course, all games are videotaped for later reference. True, all of this can be great fun for the coach and for the kids—as long as it's kept in the right perspective.

The problem is, too often the entire process becomes work, just the same as for the top professional coach who goes through a weekly regimen of reviewing game tapes, checking out the opposition, and getting to know everything about the upcoming game. If the parent/adult coach wants to do all this, well, I guess there's nothing to prevent her from doing it. But if the kids become too caught up in this frenzy the distinction between "play" and "work" becomes confused.

Keep an eye on this overly dedicated coach. Remind her that this youth sports league is not professional ball, not even college or high school ball. Sometimes you might get a rejoinder like "Look, life is competitive. And if you don't learn to prepare and to win at an early age, that's a lesson that's going to be lost on you forever."

As soon as you hear a statement of philosophy like that, be on the lookout for concerns. Chances are that no matter what kind of youth sports league your child is involved in, the basic principle of the league is to have fun first and worry about winning second.

Besides, who is the coach to appoint herself to teach and enforce the kinds of life lessons that should come from a parent? Just remember this: If you don't step in and take a stand you are basically agreeing with the coach's philosophy.

And Finally ... The Proud Parent

In just about every youth league around, the head coach of each team is allowed the pleasure of coaching his son or daughter. In most cases that's a wonderful experience for parent and child. But there are those occasions when the head coach uses his position of authority and power to make his child a top priority—and top player—on the team.

That's where problems can begin. No matter how well meaning the coach may be, when it comes to how much playing time the child gets or what position she plays, invariably the coach figures, "Well, if I'm the head coach, then I'm allowed the privilege of playing my kid when I want and where I want."

The sad reality is that if your child ends up on a team like this, there really isn't much you can do—especially if your child wants to pitch and the coach's kid happens to be a pitcher.

Occasionally, there might be that unusual parent/coach who rotates all the players to different positions so that each player, including the coach's own son or daughter, gets equal playing time. But human nature being what it is, this is the rare situation.

Try this tactic: Volunteer to act as scorekeeper for the game, and among your duties you'll also keep track of which child plays where during the course of the game. Now, in most youth leagues there is a rule stipulating that every child has to play a substantial portion of the game. That must-play rule usually stands for all types of sports and also usually stipulates that each child rotate from position to position.

So, if the head coach is the one who determines who plays where, the least you can do is keep track of playing time for the kids. In that way, during the mid-point of the game, you can gently point out to the coach who hasn't played yet and who has played the most. You should also keep track of the positions played.

Note: Even if you find that the head coach is less than thrilled with your scorekeeping, don't back down. Just make copies of the previous game's playing time and position and give copies to all team parents. After all, they're just as concerned as you are about how much time *their* own child is getting and which position he plays.

After a while it's going to be pretty obvious to all— including the head coach—that his son or daughter is doing the bulk of the pitching, is always batting first in the order, or is always the goalie or forward or whatever. And it's going to be difficult for the coach to keep this up when you have a complete record of who's playing where.

I know from personal experience that this system works. When I coached six- to seven-year-old soccer players I made it a point to juggle the lineups from period to period, rotating players. But with 14 to 15 kids on a roster, it can become quite a chore to keep track of who's played and where. Thus, I make it a point to have an assistant coach whose primary function is to keep track of each child's playing time and position played. In that way, at the end of each game I can quickly determine who, if anybody, didn't get enough time or was deprived of playing goalie or half back. And of course, it becomes a great way of fending off questions from concerned parents who feel that their little Bobby or Barbara isn't getting enough playing time. All we have to do is check the records.

Many times the head coach becomes the head coach because he suspects that his child is the best player on the team. And sometimes his philosophy becomes "The kids aren't going to have any fun if they lose all the time, and let's face it, my kid is the best we've got, so it makes all the sense in the world to play her in the most critical position."

Kids have fun only if they win? Nonsense. Remember that poll that pointed out kids would rather play on a losing team than be a bench warmer on a winning team? Nothing could be more accurate. Kids want to play; they don't want simply to applaud the accomplishments of their teammates.

If you run into a coach like this, who puts winning (and his child) as the team's top priority, make it a point to show him the results of that survey. If the coach shrugs it off with a "So what?" attitude, consider the possibility of rallying other parents of kids on your child's team to support you. After all, if the head coach is being selfish with his kid's playing time, chances are that the other parents have noticed as well and are just as concerned as you are.

What can a group of parents do to get their point across? How about staging a boycott? Simply tell the head coach that if he doesn't conform with the league's rules, then your child and several teammates are not going to show up for practice and games anymore. And if enough kids don't show up, the coach's team will have to forfeit. Believe me, if he is that concerned about his talented kid getting playing time the last thing the coach wants is for the entire team to forfeit.

Sound like strong medicine? Perhaps. But consider the analogy of school. Suppose your child were in a classroom where the teacher favored only one or two children. As a parent, would you be concerned and object to the other parents and the school? Or would you simply shrug your shoulders and say, "Well, that's too bad. I guess it's too late to make any changes...."

Two Points to Always Remember about Coaches
There are basically two concepts you have to understand about being a parent and being a coach:

- If you want to make certain your child's experience in youth league sports is a relatively pleasant one, you ought to take an active role, either as the head coach or the assistant coach. If you don't get involved, then understand that you are implicitly trusting the team's coaches to do a good job with your child.

Take an active role, either as the head coach or the assistant coach, to make certain your child's experience in youth league sports is a relatively pleasant one.

- If you discover that your child's coaches aren't doing the kind of job you would want, it's up to you to get involved. Be diplomatic in your approach. But you know your if child isn't enjoying the experience. If he comes home in tears, or you feel that his self-esteem as a player is withering, the time has come to do something.

A Checklist Of Warning Signs

Be on the lookout for these telltale signs of poor coaching skills:

- You hear obscenities being thrown around by the coach. ("Sonofabitch!" and "Goddammit" have become commonplace on the coaching lines. Amateur coaches must think that's what pro coaches do—curse loudly. Whatever these amateur coaches are thinking, the fact remains that there is never any excuse for swearing around kids.)

- The coach criticizes the player—not the player's behavior. ("You guys stink out there today!" as opposed to, "You guys are playing like you're tired today." A coach can criticize a child's behavior, but never criticize the child.)

- The coach doesn't want to hear any suggestions from the parents. ("Yeah, yeah, don't you think I know that already?" is the usual response from the know-it-all coach when given advice by a parent.)

- The coach argues and bickers with the referee, umpire, or official.

- The coach allows cheating to take place saying, "It's part of the game. Everybody does it."

- The coach doesn't allow equal playing time at all positions for all the players.

- The coach makes the mistake of allowing winning to become the driving force behind the team's play. ("Kids, if you don't win today, then we'll lose our chance for the championship next weekend!")

- The coach makes the kids feel badly when they lose and makes them feel worthy only when they win.

Your son or daughter may be lucky enough to avoid these kinds of coaches. But sadly, they're probably going to run into one sometime in their young athletic careers. Remember, nobody wants you to become a nosy, pushy parent. At the same time it's up to you to watch out for your child's welfare.

1. *The New York Times Health Magazine*, April 21, 1991, p. 26.

CHAPTER 6

Under Pressure

If there is one concern that most parents have about their kids and competitive sports at an early age, it's just how much pressure, if any, should be placed on the youngsters.

Jim Richard, a psychologist based in the Philadelphia area who has long been involved in sports, tells the story of a 13-year-old swimmer who was so dedicated to her sport that she would get up at the crack of dawn each day and go to a pool and swim laps before school. Then after school, she would head back to the pool for more practice and laps.

This pattern and dedication to her sport had become an integral part of her life. Then one day, she started to complain of some pains in her stomach. Visits to the physician didn't turn up any medical reason for the symptoms so eventually the concerned parents felt it might be a psychological problem. The parents turned to Dr. Richard.

As Dr. Richard recalls in his interviews with the girl and her parents, a theme began to develop. First, when talking with the girl about her love of swimming and her fierce desire to practice and compete, Dr. Richard asked her why all this was so important to her. Said the teenager: "Well, Mom wants me to do well."

A few minutes later Dr. Richard was interviewing the mother separately. In the course of that discussion the psychologist repeated the question as to why it was so important for the girl to work so hard at her sport. The mother replied, "Her father wants her to do well."

As Dr. Richard comments: "It didn't take too long to realize that the lines of communication regarding parental approval were not functioning too well in this family unit. The singular question remained—who is pushing this child to compete and why?"

Ultimately, through his work with the 13-year-old girl, it became clear to Dr. Richard and her family that her stomach pains were caused by a combination of stress and fatigue. Indeed, a follow-up check with the physician showed that the girl was suffering from a low red-blood-cell count, a sure sign of fatigue and an indication that she might be more vulnerable to stress-related illnesses.

Eventually, she admitted to herself that she really wanted to spend more time on her work in school and with her teenage friends socially. Normal? For a 13-year-old girl to want to spend more time with her friends and in school? Of course. But it also meant an acknowledgment from the parents that their daughter didn't want to spend all that time in the pool twice a day.

What does all this mean? Observes Dr. Richard: "Kids often times know better than their parents what they want to do. But sometimes parental approval and parental dreams get in the way—and the problems pop up in psychological ways with their kids."

Parental Pressure
This argument about parental pressure has raged since Carl Stotz threw out the first ball in Little League play back in 1939. On the one hand, some parents look upon organized youth sports as nothing more than a testing ground for kids to become adjusted to the world of hard-nosed competition. As a result kids are instructed to look upon competitive league play as a chance to win.

At the other end of the spectrum, some parents abhor the concept of competition for kids aged five through 13. To them all that matters is that the children are allowed to play. The thought of winning is so low a priority that it hardly exists at all.

What is the proper or preferred approach? And along those lines, just how much pressure should be applied to a child in terms of his wanting to win?

Too Much and Too Little
To get a better idea of how parents differ on this crucial issue, let's try to examine each point of view. For starters I asked one of my fellow coaches in an organized youth league about his reputation as a "no-nonsense coach" who taught and urged his kids to win whenever they took the field. Here was his basic philosophy:

The world is a competitive place and as a parent I feel it is my obligation to teach this fact to my children—and my players. Those who fail to recognize that reality or those who don't want to recognize it are doing nothing more than shielding their children from the truth. In the long run that's only going to hurt their children as they prepare for life in the real world. Hence, when it comes to playing youth sports, I firmly believe the kids should play for keeps, that scores be kept, and that the kids fully understand that winning is where the fun is and that losing is nowhere and painful. Because let's face it, in just a few years' time, these same little kids will be competing against each other to get into the best colleges and, ultimately, to obtain the best jobs. You might as well teach them now what life is really like; otherwise, you're just preparing them to become losers.

In contrast to the learn-to-cope-with-life-by-winning doctrine, another coaching friend of mine espouses a totally different point of view. He says:

Look, the way I see it, kids are going to learn how to be competitive on their own and will do so at their own pace. It's not my job or purpose to teach them how to be competitive or even how to win. In fact, that to me, is their parents' responsibility. I feel that it's my job to emphasize team play, fun, and a sense of accomplishment. That's not to say I don't want my kids to win—I do. But I'm sure not going to make the pursuit of victory the only reason why they're playing. Otherwise, if they lose a few games on the way they'll become discouraged and might just give up on me and the sport entirely. And yes, I know it's a competitive world out there. But to me, before you can start worrying about competing, you have to first have your priorities in order. And that's what I try to teach.

What Does This Mean to You?
What happens if you feel that your child isn't flourishing under a particular coach's style? Should you try to convince the coach to change or modify his philosophy? Well you can try, but you probably won't be very successful. After all, he already believes that his approach is the proper one. From his point of view, it's you who ought to reassess your view of youth sports.

What you *can* do is the following:

- Talk to your child. See if she enjoys playing the sport first. Then ask if she enjoys playing for the coach.

- Ask your child whether she feels she is learning any new skills from the coach. Ask your child to demonstrate some of these skills for you.

- Ask her how the other kids like playing for that coach.

The key thing to listen for when having this conversation is the amount of enthusiasm your child exhibits. In other words, she might tell you, "Yeah, it's okay. I like the team and I like the coach and so do the other kids," but you'll be able to tell from her lack of vocal enthusiasm that perhaps she is just saying these things and not really meaning it.

If you come away with a feeling that your child looks upon practice (and the games) as more of an obligation than something to look forward to, you might want to go along to a practice or two and see what happens there. Watch your child. Watch the coach. Watch how they interact with each other and the other kids. Perhaps you'll see something during the practice sessions that shows why your child isn't as enthusiastic as she should be.

What might that be? Maybe your child isn't as talented as the rest and she tends to be ignored. Maybe the other kids tease and pick on your kid. Maybe your child doesn't understand the rules of the game as well as the other children and finds herself standing off away from the action.

Checking the Level of Enthusiasm

Many coaches will take the time to check on the involvement and enthusiasm of all children at practices and games. And most of the time, they'll quickly pick up on which kids aren't truly participating.

But sometimes they don't. Perhaps the coach is only paying attention to those who show superior athletic skill and talent, figuring the other kids can find their own way to amuse themselves. Thus, just to make certain your child hasn't fallen under the influence of one of these coaches, it's vital to go to a few practices to see what's going on.

Once there, you don't have to say much; in fact, it's probably a better idea just to stand off to the side and be somewhat inconspicuous. In that way you will have a perfect opportunity to observe how your child interacts with the others. Remember, parents are the first to point out that "my child is perfect." But you can learn a lot about your "perfect" child by watching and observing her around other kids.

Objective observation is something that can't be emphasized enough. It's too bad that the coaches can't see themselves in action.

In a wonderful study that was done a few years ago, a group of youth sports coaches were asked to rate, from 1 to 100 percent, how they viewed common problems in coaching kids' sports. As a follow-up to that first question, those same coaches were asked if these typical problems applied to their own coaching experiences.

Notice the results:

**CHILDREN'S SPORTS PROGRAMS
OVEREMPHASIZE WINNING**

In general true—73%   In my program true—49%

COACHES ARE POOR LEADERS

In general true—38%   In my program true—27%

KIDS ARE PLACED UNDER TOO MUCH STRESS

In general true—49%   In my program true—31%

PARENTS FREQUENTLY INTERFERE

In general true—52%   In my program true—31%

The pattern is quite consistent and clear. The coaches always see the problems with youth sports leagues as much more prevalent with other coaches in other leagues. [1]

Parental Approval and Pressure
Remember that one of the strongest motivators for any child is striving to please one's mom and dad. In too many sports situations, the parent accidentally applies too much pressure on the child who happens to show some athletic ability. As was illustrated in the earlier chapters, it's absolutely great if your seven-or

eight-year-old shows that she happens to be a little more advanced in her soccer or swimming or baseball skills than her peers. But—and this is important —it's also up to the parents to show some adult behavior when it comes to pushing and prodding their child to maintain that level of athletic superiority.

Kids' interests can change dramatically from day to day. Today's eight-year-old soccer star might wake up tomorrow and love nothing more than skateboarding. The soccer ball will lie untouched in the corner while he spends his free moments riding a skateboard.

To many parents this might seem distressing. After all, being a soccer star can bring all sorts of desired rewards, such as popularity in school, write-ups in the local newspaper, even a college scholarship. But skateboarding? Not exactly an Olympic sport. Because of this, concerned parents find themselves saying things like "Dear, wouldn't you rather play soccer today—and let that skateboard have a day off?"

Again, be the adult here. Remember that childhood is, if anything, a time of experimentation and exploration. All you really want your children to do is to develop a sense of fun, independence, and self-confidence. So relax—today's skateboarder might grow up to be tomorrow's star quarterback or swimmer or goalie. The point is, let them have fun, try to keep your own ambitions and dreams off to the side, and let them develop and pursue their own.

Above all, don't ever make the mistake of applying pressure to your children. Let them experience the joy of winning and the frustration of losing. Don't worry— they'll pick up quickly on which of the two they prefer. Just don't make the mistake of insisting that they must win all the time. That kind of heavy pressure combined with a child's desire to please Mommy and Daddy can really cause problems down the road.

Don't believe me? Just pick up the sports pages and you'll find stories like Rob Dibble's every day.

The Rob Dibble Story
Whether you're a diehard baseball fan or someone who casually follows sports at a distance you may have heard the saga of Rob Dibble. An extremely talented major league pitcher in the early 1990s, Dibble was considered one of the top performers in the game. He was well paid for his talents and highly regarded by his peers for how hard he could throw a baseball.

Despite all these wonderful accomplishments, Rob Dibble had a problem. He had some difficulty in coping with the frustration of his chosen profession. Over a period of a few years, Dibble vented his anger in the following ways:

- April 18,1989—After an opposing pitcher got a hit off Dibble, the angry relief pitcher retaliated by throwing at the next batter on purpose.

- May 24, 1989—An opposing hitter from the St. Louis Cardinals got a hit off Dibble which allowed a run to score. Dibble was so infuriated by this development that he took the hitter's bat and threw it against the screen behind home plate in Cincinnati's Riverfront Stadium.

- April 11, 1991—Another incident in which an opposing pitcher got a hit off Dibble. Dibble threw his next pitch at the next batter touching off a major on-field brawl between the teams.

- April 28, 1991—After a less-than-satisfying outing on the mound, Dibble threw a ball out of anger that landed some four hundred feet away in the bleachers. The ball hit a woman on the elbow, bruising her and causing her great pain.

- July 22,1991 - After an opposing batter put down a perfect squeeze bunt, Dibble angrily fielded the ball and fired it right at the player as he ran down the first-base line, hitting him in the leg.

Please note that after all of these emotional outbursts, Dibble was fined by the National League and publicly apologized for his actions. Finally, after the last incident, he decided to seek psychological counseling on how to deal with his emotional frustrations.

But the questions remain—how did Rob Dibble get to this point in his life? And how many other Rob Dibbles are out there? Is it just a quirk that he can't seem to control his emotions when things go poorly for him? Or was he programmed this way?

The Pressure Growing Up
The way Rob's mother, Barbara Dibble, sees it, it's her fault that her son has difficulty in coping with the frustrations of major league baseball. According to a lengthy article in *The Hartford Courant*,[2] Mrs. Dibble once wrote in a letter to her talented but angry son. "I'm [the reason] why you're like this. I pushed you too hard," she wrote.

Reflects Mrs. Dibble: "Growing up, we wouldn't let him [Rob] fail. Looking back, I feel terrible. I'm not a horrible person but, no, we never said, 'Better luck next time.' We said, 'Rob, how come you played so bad?'"

Dibble grew up in a suburb of Hartford, Connecticut, and comes from a highly athletic family. By age eleven it was apparent to all observers that young Rob was very likely the most talented of the bunch, a terrific hitter, fielder, and pitcher. Yet, during that same time his mother and father were the recipients of a trophy from the league naming them as the "Worst Little League Parents in History."

Confrontations between Rob and his mother were loud and commonplace. Confrontations between Mrs. Dibble and Rob's coaches were also loud and commonplace. In one particular high school game Dibble had just finished racking up 17 strikeouts in seven innings when the high school coach took Rob out of the game in the eighth inning with an 11-0 lead in order to rest his arm and allow some of the substitute players to gain some on-the-field time.

After the game was over, Mrs. Dibble was in the dugout screaming and yelling at the coach for having removed her son from the game. She was angry because she felt that all the pro scouts had not seen enough of Rob's ability to throw a baseball.

When Rob had been pitching in a Little League game a few years earlier, his team was winning 15-0 when a youngster from the other team got lucky, stuck his bat out, and hit a blooper for a single. Immediately angered by this development, Dibble threw his glove down and started stalking the mound yelling and screaming. He couldn't cope with the idea that another kid could get a hit off him.

All this is not to suggest that Dibble is crazy; indeed, he is far from that, and has a lovely wife and family whom he cherishes. But when it comes to competing in the demanding sport of baseball, Dibble openly acknowledges that for some reason he has great difficulty putting things in proper perspective. "I have to mature. I have to come to grips with handling the pressure. I'm just one guy who doesn't handle it very well."

Hopefully, Rob Dibble has now come to grips with his frustrations through counseling. But you wonder how many tantrums, angry outbursts, and dangerous displays of temper he's had to endure and inflicted on others through his life—just because he was always told that he wasn't allowed to fail when playing baseball.

Remove the Stigma of Failure

While the example of Rob Dibble may be an extraordinary one, the lesson shouldn't be lost. If nothing else, it's noteworthy that despite all his fears and concerns, he has actually fought his way through the ranks and become one of the premier relief pitchers in baseball.

Of course, most parents aren't going to be too concerned if their son or daughter doesn't grow up to be a star for a major league team. They just want their children to enjoy competitive sports and to have a feeling of satisfaction and accomplishment when they do well.

That's precisely where the concept of failure comes into play. Try to keep the child's perspective in mind. From your son or daughter's point of view, it is thrilling to finally master the art of throwing or catching a ball, of kicking a soccer ball hard, or riding a bike or learning how to skate.

That sense of self-mastery is absolutely critical to the development of self-confidence, of independence and of the sense of having achieved some ability to control the world around them. To children, mastering a skill brings fun and self-satisfaction.

On the other hand, not being able to master an athletic skill brings a sense of personal frustration and to some extent, worry about personal failure. And the sense of frustration and failure becomes even more intense if the child sees other kids his or her age who are already able to master that skill.

All of these experiences and observations—again, from the child's perspective—first come into focus when they start going to school. By the time they start showing up for youth league practices, they can gauge their own abilities quite objectively against those of their peers.

To illustrate this point, take a moment to talk with your child and ask him or her about the other kids on the team. Ask your son or daughter about each child, who is a really good player and who is not. Believe me, you'll be surprised to hear a seven-year-old give you a fully detailed "scouting report" on each kid. "Jimmy's awesome, he's the best! Jennifer is good at kicking the ball too. Mike is kinda slow, but Barbara is a great goalie!"

After going through each member of the team, you might want to ask your child about herself and how she fits into the team evaluation. Again, you'll be surprised at how incredibly honest kids can be about themselves and their own abilities. They'll tell you just how good or bad they are as compared to their teammates.

This is an excellent opportunity to look into that window of your child's self-esteem. Because kids tend to be so honest about their own abilities, you'll be able to get a real feel for just how good your child thinks she is—especially as compared to other kids. Take a few moments to explore your child's game objectively with her. Ask her what strengths she thinks she has when she plays. What aspects of the sport she doesn't do well. Above all, let her talk. She'll tell you everything you want to know and then some.

Leave the Right Impression

In dealing with parental pressure and with the internal pressure that a child places on herself, it's absolutely vital that you, as the parent/adult, keep all of this in proper perspective. It's vital that you praise your child's mastery of skills, reminding her of the progress she has made and reassuring her that everybody learns things at a different rate.

What you don't what to do is leave a lingering impression with your child that she isn't keeping up with the others or that she isn't trying hard enough or even worse, point out to the child that she comes from a very athletic family. All of these seemingly innocent comments or observations can have a major and often negative impact on a youngster. Remember—your child wants to please you and will do whatever she thinks will help gain that approval. Be careful in your approach and always monitor your thoughts before you open your mouth.

What to Say To...

"The Slow Learner"

Let him know how proud you are of his accomplishments. Point out specifically an area of improvement in the skills he's mastered. Try to find one area in his game that he tends to shine in—even if it's as small as being a fast runner or knowing the rules of the game—and let him know what a great strength that is.

Don't be afraid to make a big deal out of his improvements. If you want your child to enjoy himself, make him feel as though he's making progress. And if he asks you why he isn't as good as the others, just remind him of some of the stories of famous athletes from the beginning of this book who weren't the best when they started out either. This ugly-duckling approach can work wonders for a child's desire to stay with sports and will help him maintain a sense of enthusiasm.

"The Quick Study"

If you are fortunate enough to have a child who seems to be a star among her peers, the first thing to remind her is to develop a sense of sportsmanship and graciousness if another parent, ref, or classmate compliments her play. Teach your child how to acknowledge these nice words and how to say thank you with sincerity.

Never assume your child knows how to react to these pleasant exchanges; after all, she probably has never had anyone outside the immediate family tell her how talented she is.

In the meantime you can encourage your child's abilities by always praising such on-the-field behavior as exemplary and worth striving for. For example, the child will earn plenty of self-satisfaction when she scores a goal or gets a hit. That kind of behavior you don't have to reinforce too much because your child is already getting lots of positive reinforcement, both in the achievement and in the admiration of her teammates.

Rather, you might want to spend some time telling your child how proud you are of her abilities on the playing field, and that you were particularly proud when she passed the ball to a teammate, thus enabling her to score her first goal of the season. Or how impressed you were when she volunteered to sit out for a few innings so another child who hadn't played could have a chance.

In other words, because your child is lucky enough to have mastered many of these skills, you now have a golden opportunity to get her to enhance other aspects of her social behavior as it relates to sports and sportsmanship.

Comments To Avoid

Remember when it was suggested that you monitor your thoughts before you give voice to them? Along those lines, be careful that you don't unintentionally say to a child:

- "What's wrong with you—don't you want to be as good as the others?"

- "You could have played even better if you had paid more attention."

- "You know, everyone in the family was a great athlete—me, your mom, and your older brothers."

- "Losing is no fun at all. The fun part of the sport is winning."

- "You scored two goals today. Next Saturday, I want you to score three goals."

- "Your mother and I have spent a lot of money on equipment and uniforms to let you play on this team."

Is there a common theme to these not-so-subtle parental suggestions?

All of them carry the underlying message "Don't let your parents down!" Whether it's making the kid feel guilty that money has been spent on him or that everybody in the family was a great athlete or that you can't have any fun unless you win, the point is clear. Kids pick up very quickly what their parents want them to do. It's a heavy responsibility for moms and dads to check and censor all their personal ambitions. It is difficult, but it is necessary for a child's best interests.

Observes Dr. Jerry R. May, chairman of the United States Olympic Sports Psychology Committee: "A lot of overachieving parents tend to expect overachievement in sports from their children. I've seen this even when the parents aren't or weren't athletes themselves." [3]

Dr. Salvatore V. Didato, a psychologist from Spring Valley, New York echoes, "The biggest problem a father has to contend with is his own pride. He has to watch that he doesn't push beyond reasonable limits to achieve his own unstated goals."

Living vicariously through one's children has long been identified as a common problem with proud parents. But it's a situation that can be handled as long as the parent is aware that it is a problem.

Dr. Kenneth Cohen, a child psychologist from White Plains, New York, says it's all up to the parent.

> The parent may see the kids' sports as a stepping-stone to success as an adult. The message from the parent to the child in terms of achievement can be given in a supportive way to permit the child to strive and incorporate those values in himself. In that way the child succeeds in satisfying himself as well as his parents. This produces a healthy, competitive spirit.
>
> On the other hand the parent can be punitive and judgmental, and unwilling to accept a child's limitations. This can create a tremendous amount of anger and frustration. Then there is a tendency by the child to defy the parent by failure—to use failure as a way of undermining the parent's high expectations and unreasonable demands. [4]

The Ultimate Goal

A parent, as evidenced by the observations of these psychologists, should always be conscious of how much pressure he puts on his children to perform. Ideally the child will want to play the sport because he enjoys the experience and because he is proficient at it. Nobody is going to be so unrealistic as to assume that a child is going to keep playing competitive sports just because it is good for him and his physical development. That's like expecting kids to eat spinach just because it's good for them.

Kids are too smart for that. They'll figure out their talents on their own without any prompting from their parents. That's precisely why kids should be encouraged at a young age to try all different kinds of sports. Whether baseball, football, basketball, ice hockey, swimming, gymnastics, you name it—eventually they'll find the sport or sports they enjoy and want to stay with.

What should a parent do? Encourage, enjoy, and get involved. That's all your child will ever need.

1. R. Martens, *Joy and Sadness in Children's Sports* (Champaign, Ill.: Human Kinetics Publishers, 1978), p. 310.
2. *The Hartford Courant*, June 23, 1991.
3. *The New York Times*, July 4, 1991.
4. *Rockland Journal-News* (White Plains, NY.), June 16, 1991.

CHAPTER 7

Motivating All Kids to Enjoy Sports

John Wooden is regarded as one of the greatest basketball coaches of all time. His success year after year at UCLA is legendary; indeed, during the 1960s and 1970s, UCLA won the national championship nearly every year.

Yes, Wooden knew all about winning. And with each passing season, UCLA fans began to expect more of the same from him. There was tremendous pressure on the coach. If you ask most big-time college coaches today, they'll tell you straight out that "winning is serious business" and that "there's very little tolerance for mistakes or errors" by the players.

But Wooden had a different attitude; a different message for his players. He was always stressing the positive, looking to compliment his players, and to motivate them through positive reinforcement. And when Coach Wooden did make his points, he did so in a calm, constructive fashion that was precise and specific to each player. He made certain that his words were focused on the individual athlete so that the lines of communication were clear, and the player came away motivated.

During one of his last years coaching, two psychologists decided to record all of Coach Wooden's coaching comments during UCLA practice sessions.

According to their observations close to 75 percent of Wooden's comments were precise, detailed, and specific to an individual player. Further, the comments never dealt with the player's attitude or personality; instead Wooden focused on the player's on-the-court actions only.

Those observations contained plenty of praise. The other 25 percent of Coach Wooden's comments were 12 percent requests to the team to keep hustling, 7 percent praise and encouragement to the team to achieve their goals, with only 6 percent of his coaching comments scoldings. Again, the scoldings dealt only with a player's actions not his person.[1]

In other words, 94 percent of his coaching communications were specific and full of praise and optimism. Wooden's coaching record speaks for itself. Perhaps it would be an interesting test to see what pattern the comments of your child's coach fall into. The typical youth coach is spending a lot more time criticizing than praising—and that's unfortunate, because nothing turns off a youngster faster than negative feedback.

Your Words—an Important Tool

Remember that in working with kids, the words you or the coach use are strong tools in shaping your child's attitude toward sports (and for that matter, toward school and most other childhood activities). As children try to master new skills, they are going to become occasionally frustrated at finding that their abilities take them only so far. It's at that point of frustration that the child will ultimately make a decision: Do I try to better myself at this skill or do I simply forget it and turn my attentions to other skills which I have already mastered?

This is the precise moment when good, solid, positive coaching can have its greatest potential impact on a child. Let's say that Kevin, a tall, lanky eight-year-old, shows great power when he swings and makes contact with a baseball. The problem is Kevin doesn't make contact too often. Indeed, baseball practice slows down considerably when Kevin comes to the plate because, invariably, he'll swing at several pitches before even coming close to making contact.

Kevin is old enough to realize that many of his friends can hit the ball on the first swing and, that for him, coming to bat is quickly becoming an exercise in painful public embarrassment. After all, he's a child who is obviously taller than the other kids his age, but he hasn't developed the skills yet to do what many of his peers can with a baseball bat.

Now, in the scope of greater things, this is hardly a disaster. But in Kevin's eight-year-old world, not being able to do what his buddies can do is a disaster, and Kevin's coach should be aware of this.

If handled the wrong way, Kevin will probably decide that swinging a baseball bat at a pitched ball doesn't do much for his self-esteem (after all, he doesn't make contact much). As a result, he'll certainly be less inclined than ever to work on this skill on his own. Rather, he'll just forget it and not practice at all.

As kids get older they eventually make their own decisions about which sports they want to pursue in high school. But you want your child to pick and choose his sports because they are the ones he enjoys most of all—not because he's tried everything else and failed.

Reward the Effort—Not the Outcome

Now suppose Kevin's coach took a more enlightened attitude toward his hitting. Suppose instead of rewarding the outcome of Kevin's swings he or she rewarded Kevin's efforts.

This is the first step to gaining Kevin's confidence as a coach, and also for Kevin to gain some sense of self esteem about his hitting. If the youngster isn't making contact with the ball, the coach should quickly pick up on this and make some constructive suggestions as to what he can do to correct the problem.

But just telling Kevin to "keep your eye on the ball" or "keep your bat steady" isn't enough. Oh sure, it's a good bet these comments are encouraging as far as they go, but they fall far short of providing Kevin with any personal motivation to want to improve his batting stroke.

This line of communication is what separates a good coach from a great coach. John Wooden would not only tell his player what he could do specifically to improve his play, but would also reward that player's efforts to improve with verbal praise. You see, before you can reward the actual performance by the youngster, you have to first reward the effort that she expends.

Why? Because if it's a difficult skill to master (and many athletic skills are), chances are that the child is not going to be able to master that skill on the first couple of tries. Hence, in order to keep the child motivated to want to stay at it and work toward that goal of achieving mastery of the skill, it's up to you or the coach to constantly praise and reinforce the effort that the child is putting forth. That way, if the child knows that her efforts are being rewarded with praise, she also realizes that the more effort she puts out the more praise she'll receive. And ultimately, the more effort she puts into mastering a skill, the sooner her skills will improve.

Suppose you were teaching a child to ride a two-wheeler or to ice skate. As an adult, you know that both skills take some time and practice to master. As a result you're much more likely to start out praising the effort your child makes as she wobbles on the bike or the skates rather than praising her for having already mastered that skill. The same mentality should apply to coaching kids in the youth leagues, whether it's hitting or catching a ball, dribbling a soccer ball, shooting baskets, or whatever. But sadly, it doesn't always happen this way.

Many youth league coaches simply make an immediate assessment of a player's abilities and quickly (and often carelessly) decide which ones can play well and which can't. Because these coaches are more concerned about winning, or at least putting a competitive team on the field, they are more inclined to spend time with more gifted athletes than they are with the kids who just haven't mastered the skills yet. And that's a shame, because in reaction to such treatment, kids like Kevin might simply give up the sport of baseball before they've even had a chance to improve, master, and develop their God-given abilities.

Keeping It in Perspective

Sometimes it's hard to believe, but many parents get caught up in the so-called glamour of seeing their sons and daughters heralded as star players, to the degree of simply throwing all perspective out the window and allowing the competitive juices to flow and take over.

Typical of the experience is the midsummer fascination with Little League games and the desire to take one's team all the way to Williamsport, Pennsylvania for the World Championship. In the summer of 1991, a team from Staten Island, New York reached the semi-final round of the tournament before losing. But before they did, The *New York Times* asked the coach of the Staten Island team (where the oldest player can only be twelve) what he looks for in selecting his star players:

> When our league season is over, the coaches of the six teams get together and vote to pick the top 18 players. We take those 18 candidates and have them compete against each other for 14 spots. A lot of people say there's too much pressure in this. But right from the start, we tell the parents that our goal is to make it to Williamsport and play Taiwan for the championship. We want to go to the top of the pyramid.

> We're looking for kids with the desire to play. They have to have talent, but they have to be willing to work hard too. We've dropped kids who wouldn't play certain positions or who missed practice.

Now at first blush, the excitement and enthusiasm of the Little League World Series certainly seems like fun. But read those quotes. If one of your children were trying out for that team, might you not wonder about the coach's opening statement regarding pressure, competition, and his stated goals for the team's success? It's almost as though by simply saying, "We're in this thing to win," he makes the entire process totally acceptable and psychologically sound. The same goes for the philosophy of dismissing kids from the team because "they wouldn't play certain positions."

Remember—you're dealing with twelve-year-olds here, kids who aren't even teenagers yet. I can't imagine what I would tell a twelve-year-old Little Leaguer who was cut from the team because he wouldn't play another position than the one he wanted to play.[2]

Shaping by Successive Approximation

Rewarding athletes for their efforts takes a little thought, but the results can be most gratifying—for both the coach/adult and the child.

Dr. Jim Richard has a theory called "shaping by successive approximation," which is of great value in encouraging an individual's effort to master a new skill. To better illustrate his idea, Dr. Richard describes how the process was used to improve his own golf game:

> I'm not a particularly good golfer, and as such, I went to practice with a golf instructor. He got me going with a golf club and a ball on a tee, and he started to watch me swing. Believe me when I tell you that I wasn't very good. But after a few minutes, I began to realize that the golf pro was fully accepting of everything I did with my swing. In fact, he kept using total positive reinforcement, gently praising my effort, concentration, dedication, whatever—to my golf swing. It was total positive regard for my effort, even though the results of my golf swing weren't very good.

> But that was just the first step, or stage, in this process of shaping by successive approximation. By the second practice session, he had started to make a few minor suggestions on how I could improve my swing, but did so while still praising my work and concentration to the task at hand. This continued to the third session, in which he really had me believing in myself, that a combination of my work efforts and a few minor changes in my swing were going to make all the difference in the world in my golf game.

> By the time I was done with the lessons, I felt confident in my swing, felt good about my efforts, and couldn't wait to get to a driving range to continue to work on my newly tooled swing. That's when it dawned on me that not only had the golf pro found a subtle way to get me to work on my swing, but along the way he had also made me feel good about my golf abilities, about my efforts to succeed, and that I was truly motivated or inspired to work on the skill even more.

As Dr. Richard points out:

> *What had happened was a pyramid approach to my wanting to get better with my game. He had shaped my approach to the sport by focusing his praise on my efforts, and then weaving in minor suggestions on a step-by-step basis. It's funny, but I saw the same kind of approach work at one of those baseball "fantasy camp" weeks for retired players and older fans. Richie Ashburn, the former major league great, was hitting ground balls at a man who was in his forties, a man who was not a very good athlete.*

> *But all that Ashburn did was keep hitting grounders at the man, and at the same time kept praising him and his work effort. Bit by bit all the praise and work began to pay off. By the end of the week, while the man was hardly a star fielder, he certainly had mastered the skill of fielding routine grounders and also looked forward to the challenge of fielding more.*

Dr. Richard's point is well taken. As a coach and parent, the best result you can hope for is for your child not only to master that certain skill, but to come away feeling good about him- or herself and internally eager to keep on improving that skill.

How You Can Apply This Theory

You can easily apply this theory of successive approximation with your own kids. What you need more than anything else is:

- an ability to sincerely praise your child's efforts to master the task at hand, and not worry so much about her immediate success.

- an ability to be exceedingly patient with your child, and not to try to hurry his development.

- an ability to make minor, subtle suggestions to your child about mastering the skill, while at the same time keeping your child's interests and spirits up with lots of positive regard for her work.

- an ability to help your child develop a sense of perspective on her progress. That is, try to get her to see for herself just how much progress she's made in mastering her skill. "Remember, Joanne, last year you had difficulty just kicking the soccer ball—and this year you can dribble the ball with either foot! That's tremendous progress!"

Reinforcing how much progress she's made with her athletic ability makes every child feel good about herself—and enhances her self-esteem. Remember—whether it's learning how to dribble a basketball, trying to develop a solid breaststroke, or catching a baseball, these are the keys to success—and to continued motivation.

Strengthening Their Self-Esteem

If there is one overall purpose of getting your son or daughter involved in organized youth sports, it is to enhance their self-esteem, to build their sense of self-confidence. All of the above coaching tips and techniques are aimed at doing just that. Just to review the highlights, keep in mind the following thoughts as summarized by Ruthmary Richard, a psychological counselor who specializes in building children's self-esteem (and coincidentally, Ruthmary is married to Jim Richard):

- Always treat your child with respect. Avoid making any remarks that are sarcastic, too adult in nature, or that leave the child confused about your intent or meaning.

- Always provide specific praise for the effort made. As outlined above, be precise, thoroughly encouraging, and praise the effort, not just the performance.

- Always give the child a sense of responsibility, a sense of independence and freedom to make his choices whenever appropriate. This is the essence of being a responsible parent; you have to let your child experience the responsibility of making decisions and choices in life.

- Always remember to respect the child's uniqueness. Each child is different from every other. Understand that and accept it. Just because your child wants to do things his way on the athletic field doesn't always make it the wrong way.

- Finally, always be a good role model for your child by maintaining a strong sense of self-esteem yourself. If you present yourself to your child in a healthy, responsive, responsible way, then your child will pattern her view of life upon your healthy outlook.

All of these are important points, and apply to more than just being a supportive coach/parent. Ruthmary Richard's approach cuts across all aspects of a child's development, whether it be on a playing field or in a classroom.

Question: How Do You Handle Obstreperous Kids?

You know the situation. There's always one kid on your team who just doesn't get it. No matter how hard you try, no matter how patient you are, no matter what you do, there's always that one kid who's seemingly out of control.

He's the one during practice who decides she's going to do just the opposite of what you told the team to do. Or he's the one who's always talking with his friend while you're trying to coach the others.

No matter what approach you take, you find you're just not getting through. In fact, if it were your kid, you'd be a lot more forthright with that problem child and would order some sort of punishment.

The question is—can a coach punish one of his or her players? And if you do punish a player, how is that going to affect that child's outlook toward you and the sport?

Tips on Dealing with Punishment

First off, with any discussion of punishment, keep in mind that many psychologists will tell you never to punish any child. They suggest that punishing a misbehaving child does nothing to reinforce positive behavior and, at worst, only tends to polarize the child against you.

However, not taking any kind of punitive action with an obstreperous child— especially a child in a team environment—can have negative repercussions, not only for that child, but for the entire team. You see, not only are you having difficulty with that problem player, chances are so is the rest of the team. And to make matters even more complicated, the rest of the players are watching you, as the coach, to see how you're going to handle this situation. Even kids as young as six are going to observe how you handle their disruptive friends and classmates.

This is precisely why you have to be very careful in the approach you take to handling that problem player. Here are a few thoughts to ponder as you begin to feel your blood pressure rise:

- Never punish a kid just to make yourself feel better or "to make a point" with the others. This kind of retaliatory behavior is totally unproductive and will do nothing to alter the child's behavior. If anything, it will make him even more rebellious toward you and the team.

- There really is no reason to scream or shout at your players. Shouting is usually interpreted by the kids as a form of angry retaliation and will accomplish nothing except the further alienation of that problem child.

- Always give the misbehaving kid at least one warning before you hand out a punishment. Make sure she hears the warning.

- When doling out a punishment, be careful to choose one that will have the desired impact. Keep in mind, for example, that the worst punishment a kid can endure is being kept out of the game. Ask any youngster and he'll say he would always rather run a couple of laps or do some sit-ups as his punishment than be told he has to sit out a practice session or a game.

Since you have the power to determine who will play, use that power judiciously and sparingly. During a practice session, if a child isn't paying attention to your coaching, or is too busy talking with her teammates, or just isn't being cooperative, there's nothing wrong with simply saying, "Why don't you go over to the sidelines and sit out for a while? When you feel as though you want to listen and participate with the others then you can come back. But for right now, go over to the sidelines."

This "punishment" should be administered in a calm, yet firm, voice. There's no need for screaming. And of course, always bear in mind the age of the child. Remember that a six-year-old has a much shorter attention span than a twelve-year-old. That is, if you find that your team of six-year-olds aren't paying attention to you, it's probably because you're coaching (and talking) too much and not letting the kids simply play:

- Be sure that you never punish a child for making a mistake in a game or for trying too hard. Be kind. Be patient. Kids have to be taught very carefully how to do certain things on a playing field, and as a coach you want to be in the role of motivating them, not punishing them.

- Finally, use punishment as a last resort. It should be used only when you feel that it's the only means of getting through to the child. And bear in mind that you're working with kids—not high school, collegiate, or professional athletes.

What Motivates Kids

On a larger level try to recognize that children, like adults, are motivated by their own self-perceived personal needs. And with kids those "needs" can vary greatly. For example, for some five- and six-year-olds, all that matters is not whether they win or lose, but rather that they get that new team uniform to wear. Worrying about doing well in practice or in the game is a distant thought as long as they look good in the mirror. After all, having and wearing that uniform is the essence of great fun.

At the other extreme, for some kids all that matters is winning at all costs. For these individuals the game wasn't worth playing without victory.

Ultimately, these youngsters will outgrow the utter disappointment of realizing that no matter how hard they try, they won't be able to win every game they play. But just growing up and coming to understand that isn't the point here, because these highly driven kids often fail to enjoy the sport and the competition for what it's worth. And that's a shame.

As a parent and as a coach, you're going to have to work hard to find out which are the "right" buttons for you to push (or not to push) with your child. At his next game try to stand on the sidelines and be as objective as you can. Study your child as another might see him. Make an attempt to evaluate your child's motivational scheme; specifically, does he seem compelled only to win? Does he seem to join in the fun and excitement of the game? Does your child tend to become nervous during the game, chewing his nails or showing other signs of inner anxiety? Or is your child at the other extreme, seemingly oblivious to what's going on and not really caring about the team's play at all?

The point is, there really is no right or wrong behavior with kids at play. That is the beauty of playing. But from a parental and coaching point of view, you can study your child's behavioral actions and get a decent idea of how to approach and support your child's motivational needs.

Meet Some Typical Kids

To illustrate, most kids can be divided into various classifications. For example:

"The Vince Lombardi Type"

The legendary football coach Vince Lombardi allegedly once said, "Winning isn't everything—it's the only thing." And you probably know kids like this who take winning and losing very personally.

If you have one of these types running around your house, relax. Yes, it's very disconcerting when he seems to handle every nonvictorious situation with a sour attitude and tears. But within a few months, he'll outgrow this stage. Sure, he'll still be grumpy and frustrated that he doesn't win, but ultimately he'll get the point—try as he might, he just can't win every event or game in life.

Of course, in the meantime, simply waiting for this phase to pass doesn't make your life any easier. All you can really try to do is emphasize to your youngster that what really counts is whether he had fun—that playing in the game is more important than winning or losing.

After all, if you want your child to keep coming back and playing again the following week, it's going to be vital that you provide lots of understanding and parental support.

Whatever you do, do not downplay the child's tears or be sarcastic in your approach. From your child's point of view, losing in that game is a big deal—perhaps the biggest deal in his young life. And even though to you, a fully grown adult, tears over something "as silly as a kid's game" may seem ridiculous, put yourself in your child's shoes. He really feels bad about that loss and doesn't want to be made fun of—especially by his parents.

"We'll Win Only If I'm The Star"

Sometimes a young gifted athlete will come to two sudden realizations: 1) I'm the best player on this team, and 2) We won't win unless I control the game.

Be careful with this youngster because she runs the double risk of alienating all of her teammates with her self-appointed role of "star" and might also suffer greatly if the team loses and she feels it was her responsibility.

She's the one who runs all over the field, controlling the action, making all the plays, and telling the other kids where to play. To the proud parent it's gratifying to see such a talented youngster. But for the other kids and those kids' parents, it's not so much fun.

It's important to sit down with a youngster like this and teach her the concept of teamsmanship. Let her understand that her teammates enjoy playing as much as she does, even if they aren't as talented. Remind her that the best teams of all time rarely had an individual star, but rather numerous stars. And finally, remind the youngster that whether the team wins or loses is a function of how everyone on the squad plays—not just herself.

That last point is important because you don't want the child thinking that she has the ultimate responsibility to carry the team to victory in every game.

The "Law And Order" Player

One of the main concerns that many psychologists and coaches have with organized youth leagues is that there are rigid, formalized rules of play. With most kids, as mentioned earlier, the concept of the "do-over" is well known and used often in recess pickup games.

But with organized leagues, with refs and team standings and so on, rules are imposed and enforced by the parents who run the league. That's not always such a great idea, especially with the younger players.

And with rules, comes kids' concerns about learning those rules and adhering to them. Once you start laying down rules to kids, they will live and die with them, so much so that any deviation can practically cause a child to panic: "But, Coach Edwards . . . that's against the rules! They can't do that! It's not fair!" You've heard this plea dozens of times. And with kids who think they are playing "by the rules," this situation can cause confusion, anger, and frustration because after all, most of the kids think they are playing by the rules.

Allow me to lay down my own rule. When teaching sports to young children (ages five to eight), put down as few rules as possible. The fewer and simpler the rules, the better off you're going to be. Don't worry, for example, about teaching them the intricacies of the infield fly rule or what constitutes a balk. Just let them play for goodness' sake. The rules will take care of themselves. And if all else fails, invoke the highly popular "do-over" play.

"The Uncertain Young Athlete"

Kids will play and learn organized sports at their own pace and when they're good and ready. Don't bother yelling at, cajoling, or threatening them. Just let them be.

Example: When my own son, John, was six-years-old and playing soccer in a local league, he asked his coach where to play on the field.

"You're a sweeper, John," his coach told him, "And you play right here." With that, the coach took John by the hand, picked a spot on the field in front of the goalie, and John gladly stood right there.

Problem was, John, like most kids, didn't quite understand the total field concept of soccer. So, a few minutes into the game, the ball came bounding down the field toward the goal. And on its way it went right past John, about two feet to his left.

But John stood his ground and didn't dare move from where his coach had told him to stand. Sure enough the ball rolled by John and kept going. He could easily have kicked it, but he thought he was thoroughly following the coach's instructions.

As expected, John said that his job was sweeper and that he had been told exactly where to stand. And stand he did, for the entire game; he didn't move from that spot, no matter how close the ball came.

It's a cute story, but you get the idea. If John had been playing in a kids' pickup game or at recess, he never would have just stood in one spot. But once the rules and regulations of the organized soccer league were put forth, he simply did what he was told. Literally.

By the following year, when John was seven, he knew how to play the game of soccer. And when he thinks back on the stationary strategy of his first game, he realizes how funny it was. But remember— it took him an entire year to learn the game and to grow with it.

"Alibi Ike" Syndrome

Saving face is just as important for kids as it is for grown-ups. Just as you're tempted to make up an excuse for missing a putt or making a bad shot on the tennis court, so are kids.

The difference is that most adults don't voice their alibis or excuses, whereas kids do. Again, when your child tells you that "the sun got in my eyes" or "I wasn't ready" or "I had called time out," or whatever excuse he comes up with, don't be alarmed. And don't take issue with his excuse.

If you start accusing him of making up silly excuses, all you're going to achieve is an argument and perhaps tears or disillusionment. Instead, gently remind your child that excuses are not really well liked in sports and that as he gets older, he'll begin to understand that alibis and excuses will not be well received by their friends either.

Don't worry. Your child will hear you. Explain this to him in a calm, quiet manner. And if he insists on manufacturing more excuses, that's fine for the time being. But every time he gives an excuse in the future, just remind him that eventually, people aren't going to appreciate that kind of response.

As with most kids' concerns about winning in sports, just give him some time and patience.

1. R. Martens, et al., *Coaching Young Athletes* (Champaign, Ill.: Human Kinetics Publishers, 1981), p. 33.
2. *The New York Times*, August 24, 1991.

CHAPTER 8

Working with the Athletically Gifted Child

Let's face it. Some kids—because they're bigger, stronger, faster, or they develop neuromuscular coordination at an earlier age—tend to be better athletes than their classmates.

You know who they are. They're the kids who dominate the game's action, no matter what the sport. Invariably they're the ones who are always around the activity on the field. Or if it's a swimming meet or gymnastics competition, they're the ones who win all the events and ribbons.

The point is—dealing with star athletes is also a part of working with kids in youth sports leagues. But as you might imagine, dealing with a "star" brings with it a unique kind of agenda, especially for the parent and the coach.

Meet Mike, Star Athlete on Your Team

Mike is nine-years-old, and everybody in your athletic community knows who he is. Ever since he was six and played in his first soccer, baseball, and ice hockey games, it was clear he was a cut above the rest of the players. In soccer, when the other kids were trying to learn how to kick a ball, he was already dribbling the ball downfield and kicking it hard into the goal—with either foot.

It was a similar story in baseball. Other kids were just learning how to swing a bat and make contact, when Mike was already drilling shots around the ball park. In ice hockey, while other kids were barely able to stand up on skates with their equipment on, Mike was able to skate sharply both forward and backward.

Everybody in the community—including the parents, coaches, and kids—knew about Mike. Coaches knew that whichever team he played for, that team became an immediate threat in every game it played— because of Mike's presence. Furthermore, the coaches Mike played for recognized how superior he was, and once scores became lopsided, Mike was always the first child to be benched so that other, lesser-developed teammates could play.

This pattern stayed with Mike through ages six, seven, eight, and nine. With each passing year, while other kids continued to grow and improve their own athletic skills, so did Mike. He not only kept pace with their growth, he surpassed it.

None of this was lost on Mike's parents. Both had been good athletes as kids. It was clear that being around two older brothers who were also good athletes helped Mike develop and improve his athletic skills at a faster pace than did his classmates.

You Make the Call
Now, let's assume you've heard about this youthful, wunderkind athlete and have even seen him play once in a while. But you really never got to know him because he played on other teams in the league.

But this year surprise! — you're going over the list of players on your soccer team and there's Mike's name at the top of your list. You're immediately excited because let's face it, with Mike on the team, you know you're probably going to win a lot of games.

With that kind of enthusiasm, you call for the first practice. Saturday morning bright and early, you introduce yourself to the team. But wait—while you're giving the team rules for the season, you notice that your star player is not even there. In fact, he shows up about fifteen minutes late. You politely confront Mike and he tells you without any hint of apology, that he overslept, and besides, why should he bother having to be on time for practice in the first place?

This bothers you but you look past it. After all, Mike is a talented player. But the next week, he doesn't show up at all. You call him at home; he says he's sick. The next week is the first game. You tell the team to assemble at 11:45 for a noon game. Everybody gets there on time except Mike. He arrives at 11:58 and immediately takes his position on the field without even reporting to you first.

In the first quarter of the game, Mike scores a goal and dominates play. In the second quarter you shuffle the lineup, letting the others who sat out the first quarter get a chance to play. You tell Mike to sit down for a quarter. He mutters something obscene directed at you, sulks off to the side, and then during halftime is seen talking to members of the other team. At the start of the second half, he plays again, this time scoring two goals. But on the second goal, rather than celebrating, he rudely mimics the opposing goalie.

Having seen enough for one day, you bench Mike for the fourth quarter. With a few minutes left to go in the game you turn around to see what Mike is doing and there is no sign of him; indeed, his teammates tell you that he's left to go home.

That night you decide to call Mike's parents who were in attendance at the game. Before you even start the conversation in an adult, polite way, Mike's father is all over you, questioning your ability to coach and accusing you of getting in their son's path to stardom. Finally, just before the phone slams down, you hear, "You know what the problem with people like you is? You're a loser—and you perpetuate your losing ways on other people's kids. And to me that's not fair either to my kid or to the other children on the team." Now after your blood pressure begins to settle down again, answer the following questions. If you were in this situation, would you:

A. Have a long talk with Mike and tell him that he has to learn a sense of fair play and teamsmanship if he ever wants to be a true champion?

B. Call the league commissioner the next day to see if you can get Mike transferred to another team in the league?

C. Let the situation be and try to put up with Mike's actions, because after all, his parents certainly feel his behavior is more than acceptable and who are you to interfere with the way a mom and dad want to raise their child?

Sadly, children like Mike are more common than you think, and the answers to the above queries aren't as cut and dried as you might think. However, let's take the answers one by one.

Following response B—transferring the kid to an other team—solves nothing except to make Mike somebody else's problem. True, it gets rid of your ongoing headache (along with your star player), but you really haven't chosen the most responsible route.

As for answers A and C—well, there's the hard choice. On one hand, with choice A, as the coach of the team you have a responsibility not only to Mike but to the other kids to lay down the law with your rules about timeliness, sportsmanship, and so forth. You then have to have the guts to stick to those rules and enforce them. If you select choice C, you continue to allow Mike to keep pulling his selfish stunts—and gradually the other players on the team will lose respect for you. Kids may not be familiar with the term double standard, but they'll certainly understand the concept, as in "Hey, Coach, how come Mike doesn't have to come to practice and he still gets to play?"

So, response A is your best choice even though it's obvious that Mike's behavior patterns are not going to change much if his own parents are telling him at home to ignore his "wimpy, losing coach."

And for better or worse, you have to remember that Mike's parents are precisely that—his parents. It's their right to teach their child how to play sports, about being self-centered or being a team player, about being on time, and about having responsibility and respect for others. If Mike's parents don't want to teach him those social rules, fine—that's their choice. Unfortunately, as much as you disagree with their philosophy, you still have no right at all to interfere with those parental choices.

Walking a Fine Line

So what's the answer? Simple. You have to walk a fine line. Take a few moments one day when Mike and his parents are together at a game or practice. In a calm, adult manner, explain to them all that "as coach, I have to set down certain rules and regulations, not just for my own son or daughter but for everyone on the team. And my rules are quite simple. All the kids, including Mike, certainly have the ability and intelligence to follow them.

"But, like any coach of any team, if someone doesn't obey my rules, I have a simple response: they don't play. It's as simple as that. I have a responsibility to all the kids and to all the parents to teach and reinforce team play and sportsmanship. Now, of course, I want Mike to play on my team. But by the same token, I want to make it very clear to you all that these are my rules. If you have any questions, let's get them out in the open right now. Otherwise, if there's no problem, I will expect Mike to be just like everybody else on the team. I do not allow any double standards on my team."

At this point you can lay out the rules. Make them simple so that any nine-year-old will understand them. If you really wish to drive home the point, have your team rules printed on three-by-five index cards so that they can be handed out to all of the team members and their parents. From there, address any concerns that Mike's parents may have. And just to reinforce your point, once again remind them that it's great that Mike is so talented, but talent or not he's going to be treated just like everyone else on the team.

It goes without saying that once you have had this interaction with Mike and his parents, it's also up to you to fully penalize anybody on the team (not just Mike) who does not follow the team rules. And if and when the time comes that Mike breaches one of your team rules, you'll have to have the guts to bench him.

The Worst Punishment of All

Remember this: The worst punishment you can hand out to a player at any age is to bench him. Worse than making him run extra laps, carry the equipment, or making him do sit-ups, the absolute worst punishment you can give a kid is to tell him that he's not going to play.

So, use that punishment wisely. It should only be used as a last resort, because there is nothing more you can do to crush a child's dreams than force him to sit out a game. But if the situation warrants drastic action, have the courage to do it.

"But that's stupid," a parent may protest. "After all, if you punish your best player by keeping him on the sidelines, you're punishing, not only him, but the entire team. Why not make him pick up trash after the game or run extra sprints? Don't keep him out of the game."

A typical parental argument, but a faulty one. If you really want to enforce a sense of team play and sportsmanship in your players, you had better teach them at an early age that team rules are meant to be followed, not broken. It might be a painful lesson for Mike and the team, but one thing is for sure—neither Mike nor any of his teammates will break any of your rules again, because they know that you mean business and that you'll bench them.

Discipline from Kids to Big Leaguers

Sports fans today often wonder why our current professional and collegiate stars have such difficulty following the simplest requests—being on time for curfew, refraining from alcohol or drug use, respecting others, and so on. In too many cases today's athletic stars were just like our nine-year-old Mike when they were growing up, but their youth league coaches opted not to reinforce team rules and regulations. Coach after coach made excuses for the star player and his selfish behavior. As a result, what we have today is the multimillionaire professional player who cares only about his own performance and not a whit for his teammates or his team's success.

True, I'm generalizing to make a point about children learning team play and a sense of discipline. But there's a great deal of truth in this explanation. If you don't believe me, pick up any sports page any day of the year and you'll read story after story about today's stars who have come to personify this type of egocentric problem athlete.

If You're the Parent of a Star

What do you do if your son or daughter happens to be one of those kids who is terrific on the playing fields? Shower her with endless praise and encouragement? Or do you try to keep your enthusiasm in check and develop a more low-key attitude toward your child's stellar play?

In general, you want to behave in a manner appropriate for your child. That is, if your child does happen to be the star on the team you'll want to show just how proud you are of her and her skills. There's certainly nothing wrong with that—so long as it's kept in perspective. That means that you, as the adult/parent, have to remember that while it's great to get excited about a child's athletic performance, you also have to remember that your child is only eight-, ten-, or twelve-years-old.

Remind yourself that your son or daughter is not playing in the World Series, Super Bowl or Wimbledon, but in the local Pee-Wee football league or town recreation tennis tournament. Be proud of her accomplishments, encourage her as much as you want, but throughout all of this competitive activity, it's up to you to maintain an adult perspective.

Warning: Once you let your enthusiasm get out of hand, you've gone beyond the scope of good common sense in parenting and coaching your child. This is particularly common with the parents of the talented young athlete. With visions of athletic fame dancing in their heads, the parents "recognize" their child as an athletic "prodigy" and then steer their entire lives around the child's development of a professional career. But as is often the case, either the child's abilities wane over time or the child just plain gets tired of totally dedicating her efforts to one activity all the time.

But the biggest problem still remains the parent who can't wait to help his child become the next Dwight Gooden or Orel Hershiser. Dr. Frank Jobe is the world's leading sports orthopedic surgeon, and most of his patients are well-known major league pitchers who suffer from arm troubles. Dr. Jobe, who ought to know about the cause of arm problems, says that the biggest source of young arm injuries is overenthusiastic parents of Little League pitchers.

Dr. Jobe explains that the parent sees his child as a top pitcher in Little League, gets him to throw more and more, and ultimately injures those tender, still developing arm muscles. "Where you get into trouble is with the parent who says, 'My kid has really got talent and I'm going to show him how to do this.' So they [the parents and the child] go back home and practice two more hours. The kid is not throwing six innings a week; he's throwing the equivalent of 15 or 20."[1]

So, again, how can you be certain that your behavior will reward and encourage your child's performance without going overboard? Here are a few simple guidelines to remember:

- *Praise Your Child—But Let Him Do The Bulk Of The Talking*

  Praise your athletically gifted child for his achievements, but don't get carried away. During a quiet time (perhaps right before bed when he's tired and you have his full attention), you can review with him his day's performance. Let him relive the thrill of his day in the sun: "Say son, remember that hit you made in the first inning? It was a line shot right into the outfield! Was that exciting for you? How did it feel?"

  Let the child describe all the action—and all of the residual emotions that filled his body. Rather than providing the play-by-play yourself, allow your little athlete to do the talking. Don't worry—given the chance with you as a sole audience, your child will chatter away with his own sense of pride and self-esteem.

  Just make certain you pay attention to what's being said. Children will only feel good about themselves when they know that Mom and Dad are riveted to their conversation, hanging on their every word.

- *Don't Set Unrealistic Goals*

  While it's fine to review the day's action, do not make the mistake of setting false or unnecessary goals for the child. Be careful of suggesting, "You were great today, scoring three goals—and I can't wait until next Saturday. I'll bet you'll score four!"

  While that kind of parental enthusiasm sounds innocent enough, remember that children tend to hear things quite literally.

- *Teach Sportsmanship*

  After going over how terrific your child was, always take a few moments to discuss the concept of sportsmanship. Your child will be much more receptive to hearing about how one should act graciously, after she's heard how well she has played.

Don't take anything for granted. Explain to her that when other parents, coaches, or players congratulate her on her play it's important to acknowledge those compliments and to be a gentlewoman about accepting such nice words of praise.

Again, be gentle with both praise and criticism. A gifted child will be less open to criticism. "After all, didn't I just score three goals in the game?" Therefore, start the conversation with something like "You know Susan, Mom and I were real proud of how you played today. But you know what made us even prouder? The way you conducted yourself after the game, making certain to tell all of your teammates how well they played. That's the kind of behavior that champions are known for."

Again, just a simple matter of building upon one positive experience, getting her attention, and then using parental approval pressure to urge her to be more sensitive to others' need for self-esteem.

This approach is particularly helpful when the gifted youngster realizes that not only is she outstanding, but that lots of her teammates are either average or below average in ability. In many cases the gifted athlete may not only have little patience with the lesser athlete, but may sometimes actually be downright nasty.

There's nothing wrong with sharply rebuking the gifted athlete's caustic remarks or attitude toward her lesser teammates right on the field. That's a start. But the best time to teach sportsmanlike behavior is during that quiet time when she is much more receptive to a heart-to-heart chat with Mom and Dad. That's the time to bring up the notion that you're proud when she plays well, but even prouder when she's considerate of her friends and teammates. Use parental approval in a positive fashion. It will work wonders.

Placing The Gifted Athlete Against Older Competition

There's always the issue of whether a highly talented athlete should be moved up in classification. That is, whether a gifted nine-year-old, who easily dominates play in his age bracket, should be allowed to play with ten- and eleven-year-olds.

There is no real conclusive scientific or psychological literature on this point, but there is plenty of debate. On one hand, the theory goes that the talented nine-year-old will only benefit from playing against older and presumably more talented kids. But on the other hand, taking a nine-year-old who enjoys the solid self-esteem of being a talented athlete and putting him in a more demanding environment with older kids might be devastating.

My own personal belief is that you should be extremely cautious. Look at it this way: If the child is reaping lots of positive self-esteem from playing against his peers, why jeopardize those good feelings? After all, in another year or two, the child will continue to grow and continue to develop anyway—so why push it? Especially at such a young age.

Maybe when they reach the age of 13 or 14, they should compete against older players. But when they're still in elementary school? What's the rush?

A Typical "Star" Story
What happens when proud parents lose track of who's the adult and who's the kid?

A friend of mine tells the story of a boy who was the star performer on his Little League team. Ever since he was six-or seven-years-old, he had been a little bigger, a little stronger, and a little more athletically gifted than his buddies. Thus, when he got to Little League, he immediately became one of the top players.

The parents, understandably, were quite proud of their son's achievements. Friends and teammates idolized him and always counted on him to come through in the clutch. For his part, the boy certainly enjoyed the adulation (who wouldn't?), and fully embraced the role of star athlete.

Secretly the parents couldn't wait until the boy reached high school. By then, they assumed he'd really become a superstar and they fantasized about college scholarships, maybe even a professional contract from a major league team.

At dinner and whenever they could, the proud parents would praise their son for his athletic achievements. His dad would ask him all the time about which major league team he would like to play for. His mom would gush about how proud she was of him and how much she loved seeing his name in the local paper whenever he was the star in the Little League game. All in all, Mom and Dad made it very clear to their boy that they couldn't have been prouder of him—and that they couldn't wait until he got older and into high school to really show off his abilities.

But when the boy reached the age of 13, he was playing a game one afternoon when he slid into a base and fractured his ankle. The foot had to be placed in a cast, and the boy couldn't play ball for several weeks.

Something happened during that time he wasn't playing. While he was forced to sit by on the sidelines and heal, his friends and teammates were able to keep playing and develop their own skills. Hence, by the following spring when he was healthy again, while the boy was still regarded as being one of the better players, it was also clear that some of his teammates had shot up in height over the summer, others had gotten stronger, and others had developed even better and more—polished athletic skills.

In other words, through no fault of his own, the boy who had been the star for several years in Little League was now just another good player. The other kids were beginning to catch up to him in ability and even surpass him.

Just Another Good Player
All of this, of course, did not go unnoticed by the boy. Not knowing how to cope, over the next year or so, he began to lose interest in baseball. Sure enough, by the time he was a sophomore in high school, he came home one day and told his parents that he really didn't like baseball all that much anymore, and that he'd rather spend his afternoons doing something else.

"Are you sure?" queried the disappointed parents. "After all, you're a terrific player."

"Yeah, I'm pretty sure. Maybe I'll change my mind and play again next year."

But the boy never played baseball again. And to this day his parents will tell you that if he hadn't broken his ankle when he was 13, he would have grown up to become a star player in high school and in the pro ranks.

Better Not to Have Competed?
The parents' view notwithstanding, the truth here is that the boy's injury really had very little negative impact on his "career." All that actually happened was that the other kids in his class "grew up" and developed their own athletic skills.

In essence, it wasn't that the boy's broken ankle slowed down his growth; rather, it was just that he matured physically at an earlier age than many of his classmates. Thus, while it may have appeared to him and his parents that the injured leg cost him a great high school and perhaps pro career in baseball, the fact of the matter was that his abilities were close to peaking out when he was 13 or 14 years old, while his peers were just beginning to blossom.

Furthermore, when the boy himself began to realize that his once superstar status was quickly being surpassed by other kids, he tried to save face by deciding not to play baseball anymore. This saved him the "embarrassment" of not living up to his parents' expectations. In a sense, for this young athlete it was better not to have competed than to have competed and failed.

Holding Their Interest
The above story occurs much too often. And the parents shake their heads in disbelief, because they thought they did everything they could to make their young "star" player into a future star. After all, they showered him with love, praise, and affection. They were thrilled to see him find his place in the athletic spotlight and naturally, wanted him to stay there through high school and beyond.

As a result, they were crushed when their gifted son turned his back on baseball and walked away.

This boy's early development was a cruel trick to play on a child and his adoring parents. But the sad facts show that it happens often. Remember one of the telling statistics from earlier in this book: that only one out of every four bona fide star players in Little League ever ends up being a star on a high school team. That means 75 percent of those who excel in their preteen years are going to be just average or a little bit better than average by the time they get to their junior or senior year in high school.

On the other hand, remember that Michael Jordan wasn't good enough to make his high school basket ball team until he was a junior.

So it's plain to see that the "gifted" athlete is indeed difficult to divine. Especially at an early age. That's precisely why as parents, it's up to you to keep your child's athletic development in his preteen years on an even emotional keel.

Question: What Do You Do with the Kid Who Insists on Winning All the Time?
A friend of mine told me the other day that it's driving her and her husband bonkers that their eight-year-old son has decided that he always has to be first in every thing. First in line, the absolute best at activities, the fastest when doing assignments in school, and of course, first picked and always on the winning team at recess and on organized youth teams.

Indeed, whenever their boy doesn't come in first, tears and a tantrum soon follow. No matter how much the parents try to counsel their boy with "That's okay—nobody wins all the time," or "All that matters is that you had fun—winning isn't the important thing," they just can't seem to stop the boy from his burning drive to win all the time.

First, the good news. This kind of win-at-all-costs syndrome is quite common, especially with athletically oriented kids. Winning brings them a fleeting sense of boosted self-esteem, personal satisfaction, and instant gratification. Even a bit of self-power.

And while you should continue to remind your child that all that matters is having a good time, you should also remind yourself that your son's seemingly compulsive competitiveness is only a minor phase. Eventually (and usually within a year), he will come to realize himself that no matter how hard he tries, he won't always be number one in every activity he pursues— that somebody in his class is going to be taller, faster, spell better, sing better, run faster, or do something better than he does.

This is just a part of growing up. And while your child may not be thrilled by the discovery, he will eventually come to grips with it—just as everybody else does. Oh, he might still harbor his burning desire to be number one, but he will begin to find his own personal, selected avenue of innate talent that will allow him to pursue new goals.

In the meantime, just keep reinforcing to your child that the competitive chase itself is often much more rewarding than reaching the finish line and victory. While he might not understand that concept at first, he will catch on sooner or later. As a responsible parent, that's all you can do.

1. *USA Today*, April 19, 1991.

CHAPTER 9

Your Child's Body and Mind

Over the past few years, a tremendous amount of attention has been paid in popular sporting literature to children's performance anxiety as well as to sports injuries to kids.

At some point in your child's young sporting career, chances are that you will encounter one of these problems, and most likely both. But such difficulties are normal and to a certain extent to be expected. For example, it's usually easy to see how your child reacts to the "big game" that's to be played in just a few minutes. Some kids will bite their fingernails out of nervous anxiety. Others find that they have to urinate frequently before game time. Others find themselves chattering out of nervousness, or even yawning—not because they're tired, but as a way of fending off nerves. In more extreme cases some kids may actually have difficulty sleeping the night before a game or will not have an appetite.

For many parents, observing this kind of anxious behavior in their child can be distressing. But, rather than try to erase it, understand that most of these symptoms express simple nervous energy. Your best bet is to reassure your child that she will play well and that as long as she has fun and enjoys herself, there's little to worry about.

There are, unfortunately, other extreme situations in which a child allows the anticipation of the game to seemingly overtake her life. The sense of equilibrium regarding the upcoming game has been lost, and it's up to the parent to sit down with the child and squarely confront the issue at hand. Again, this tends to be a judgment call, but the vast majority of kids look forward to the "big game" with a positive mix of happiness, expectation, and a solid dose of nervous energy thrown together.

Nervous Nellies
If you suspect that your child is too excited, worried, or upset about an upcoming game, make certain you do two things: One, don't you get overly excited about the game and two, make certain you talk with your child right away.

Keep in mind that kids take their behavioral cues from their parents. Sometimes when a ten-year-old or twelve-year-old sees how seriously Mom and Dad are taking the game—"Hey, all we gotta do is win on Saturday and we go to the state semifinals. So, make certain you practice hard this week because you had better be ready for Saturday"—she begins to realize her "game" is not a game, but rather an event of significant importance to Mom and Dad. The child quickly figures out that if her parents are taking the upcoming game pretty seriously, then maybe she ought to take it pretty seriously too.

You can see the pattern begin to evolve. Mom and Dad didn't mean to put any pressure on the child, but even with the best intentions, it can happen—and does all the time. Before too long the child's nervousness begins to show in a variety of ways and the parents end up trying to figure out why their little athlete is always so nervous before the next game.

As you can see from this typical example, the nervous energy was not something that the young athlete was born with. Rather, she developed that pregame anxiety as a response to her parents' expectations and hopes for that game. In other words, if you lessen the unintentional pressure on the child, she will exhibit less nervous energy.

When your child shows signs of being nervous about a sporting event, listen to her worries, deal with them directly, and try to assuage her fears about winning or losing. After all, at these tender ages (usually between eight and twelve), a child can quickly equate her sense of self-esteem and self-worth with how she performs in athletic competition. That's something you do not want to happen in your child's ego development.

Remind your child that no matter who wins or loses the game tomorrow, she still is a terrific person with wonderful athletic abilities, is a hardworking teammate, and is a delight as a child. Try to make the child understand that there's a tremendous distinction between the game's outcome and what kind of person she is.

Remember, from a child's perspective, winning or losing is a big deal. Play is work to a child. And when kids get to the point where they know how to keep score and keep track of their own and their team's on-the-field accomplishments, you cannot dismiss their involvement as mere "child's play." Because to them it's not.

Pumped Up

Every parent knows about how the body will rise to a challenge, usually by releasing a rush of adrenaline into the bloodstream that pumps up the heartbeat and readies the body for action. Ask any kid about "being psyched" for a game, and he will describe to you that rush. He may not be able to tell you what the rush is, but he sure knows the feeling.

Top performers in all fields will tell you that this surge of nervous energy becomes their ally just before they take the field; they don't want to suppress or mitigate it. In other words, whereas some kids (and their parents) try to ignore that rush of adrenaline, almost all top athletes eagerly look forward to the sweaty palms, the quickened breathing, and the tightened nerves right before the game as a sign that they're now ready to perform. They actually see the adrenaline rush as a signal that it's time to compete.

Under Control

This is not to suggest, of course, that every child knows how to deal instinctively with athletic stress. There are even professional athletes who have difficulty coping with it. One major league pitcher I've worked with, for example, told me that he gets so "pumped" for a game that long after the game has been played he lies awake, his brain and body still focused on his performance.

So the question remains: If big leaguers have a difficult time dealing with pressure, what can parents teach their kids?

In a word, visualization. One of the more commonly used methods of reducing stress in adults, visualization can certainly be taught to children.

You may have heard visualization referred to as "imaging," as "self-hypnosis," or by some other name. No matter what it's called, it's fairly simple in its logic, application, and science. Fundamentally, it's a way of training one's conscious brain to "see" actions in one's mind's eye, impressing them so clearly on the brain that the rest of the body simply follows suit during times of heightened anxiety.

Let me try to clarify. Certainly you have heard of top athletes "choking" in the clutch, missing an easy shot in basketball, an easy putt, or not making a routine play during the heat of athletic battle. When these "choking" events occur, it's usually because the performing athlete has allowed negative thoughts to seep into his mind ("I'm going great so far, but what if I miss this three-foot putt?"). Unless blocked out of one's brain, negative thoughts can actually interfere with one's performance like a self-fulfilling prophecy of doom.

By eliminating all of those negative thoughts, one is far more likely to execute the routine plays, even under tremendous stress. Visualization serves exactly that function. And with children the sooner you start teaching them this ability to accentuate the positive, the better they'll be able to perform—not just in the world of athletics but in all kinds of stressful settings—taking tests in school, making speeches in class, and so on.

Visualization: How It Works
Think of the body as nothing more than a collection of muscles, bones, and nerve fiber. Without the brain telling it what to do, the body is incapable of performing. That's a given.

So let's assume you can train the mind to think only positive thoughts, to see yourself only as succeeding, doing well even in times of adversity. Again, pro athletes do this every day to sharpen their mental focus and reduce moments of stress from their game. With kids all you have to do is tell them—right before they go to sleep while they're lying in bed—that if they happen to think about the game tomorrow, just to see in their mind's eye the game being played and themselves playing well. Tell them to "see" themselves in their mind as though they were watching themselves on television.

Here's the important part. Tell your child to see herself doing well, making all the plays, being one of the best players on the field. Do not let her see herself making any mistakes or errors. Rather, tell your child to see herself in great detail executing all of the things she has been practicing perfectly in her dreamlike state.

"Honey, there's no question you're going to have fun tomorrow. After all, you've practiced very hard and you know that you're good. So if you think about the game, just imagine how well you want to play. See yourself doing everything you've practiced, and doing well. See yourself succeeding and then as you fall asleep, you'll know that you'll sleep soundly and wake up refreshed, knowing that you're ready to play."

Within a few minutes, of course, your child will begin to doze off. But before she falls asleep, she will have set the stage in her mind for a top-rate winning performance. She will be training her mind to have fun, to succeed, not to fail or disappoint herself during competition.

What does this training accomplish? First of all, it's a terrific idea to get one in the habit at an early age of thinking positively about challenges in life. There's an entire field of literature to show that motivated, positive, optimistic people tend to enjoy life, are more successful, and live longer and healthier lives than those who are pessimistic and worry about meeting challenges.

Second, by imagining oneself performing well, one is basically "rehearsing" for the upcoming game. Thus, during critical moments your son or daughter won't give in to a sense of anxious panic. Why? Because they have already in their minds "seen" themselves handle this kind of adversity, and they handled it flawlessly. And remember, the body follows what the brain tells it to do.

Be Careful of Parental Expectations
There's just one warning that comes with teaching your child visualization skills. Don't fall into the trap of placing all sorts of specific goals onto your child. Don't suggest to your child that, "Tomorrow honey, you ought to see yourself scoring at least five goals in your ice hockey game."

By doing that, you have actually increased the stress on your child because now, rather than just planning on playing well, she knows that Mommy or Daddy won't be pleased unless she scores five goals or more. If the game comes and goes and she doesn't score a lot of goals, she'll be disappointed and feel that she let you down.

Building self-confidence and a feeling of success is what visualization teaches. Indeed, if you read the autobiography of any top leader, whether from sports, business, medicine, education, or industry, chances are that the individual always had a clear vision of what he wanted to do in life. He saw himself succeeding in his chosen profession. In effect, he developed visualization skills on his own and had done so from an early age.

Day-of-the-Game Jitters
While it is not too common in the earlier age groups, sometimes kids who are ten and older will experience a serious case of pregame jitters. These kids are so "psyched" to play the game that they become restless, can't drink or eat, and in some cases their hands and fingers tremble with nervous anticipation.

Let's take the most extreme case, that of the trembling hands and fingers. Most kids are embarrassed by it. Too many of them (and their parents as well) look upon this phenomenon as expressive of fear.

Fear has nothing to do with it. These kids are so pumped up and ready to play that their body has churned out too much adrenaline. Before the physical release of this nervous energy out on the playing field, this surge of excess adrenaline causes a shaking sensation.

I have worked with a number of professional baseball players who experience these same symptoms. Once I explain to them that it's not a case of "bad nerves" or "fear of failing," but just their body indicating that they're ready and eager to get the game going, they look forward to it. They now know that it's their body's way of indicating that they're ready to go. The same philosophy should be explained to younger athletes as well. Let them know what's going on inside of them, and that these are good, positive physical symptoms— not symptoms of fear or weakness.

Fun First

One of the amazing ironies about top athletes is that the ones who seem to enjoy the game the most also seem to be the most successful. Actually, this is not a curiosity but a reality—and something that as a parent you can help your kids with.

Once your child has practiced long and hard, the game should be looked upon as a joyful, fun experience—not as a test of her grit, stamina, and competitive fire.

Perhaps you are already familiar with the concept of "flow." This is a mental or psychological state that almost all people have experienced at one point or an other in their lives. Flow is the sensation you experience when you're so involved in what you're doing and having so much fun with the task at hand that you seem to lose yourself in that activity, losing track of time, outside distractions, and other daily worries or concerns. Usually, by the time the task at hand is completed, a typical response is "Oh, look at the time! I can't believe the hours just flew by!"

"Creative flow" is a state in which the mind and body are working together toward the same goal, barring distractions. At this time people tend to be at their sharpest, both mentally and physically, and often do their best work.

Top athletes strive for this insulated state of mind and body. As a spectator you might see flow at work when a tennis pro hits ace after ace or when a baseball pitcher gets into a groove and every pitch is a strike right where he wants it. In times like these, the athlete will tell you he is so tuned in to what he is doing that he isn't even aware of outside influences or even such large, distracting noises as the roar of the crowd.

Even better, after experiencing this state of flow, the athlete will tell you that his game had never been better, and that, more significantly, he experienced no stress at all. Rather, it was all pure fun and joy to be competing.

Now, it's a bit much to expect your children to understand the concept of creative flow, but it does give your child a spiritual and psychological lift if she is taught she will always play her best merely by trying to enjoy herself out on the playing field. That may sound a bit whimsical, but I guarantee that whenever you read or hear the account of a top athlete who has just given a terrific performance, she'll always put forth the same message: "I was just trying to have some fun out there." It's an important message, because too many coaches tell kids just the opposite: that the more success you have, the more fun you'll have.

Remember, make it fun first.

Their Own Worst Enemies

Kids who play sports in their youth learn as they develop their athletic skills to trust their own instincts and athletic abilities. Still, when times get tough in the course of a game, young athletes will sometimes begin to doubt their ability. Perhaps, they'll lapse into a bad habit, one they had worked to correct through weeks of practice. Or maybe they'll just let the anxious pressure of the moment get to them and find themselves unable to perform up to their usual standards.

If you ever see your child go through this, first tell him to relax and then assure him that all athletes go through this kind of stress. For example, Jim Abbott, the talented pitcher for the California Angels, knows that when things get tight in a game, he tends to "tighten up" under the pressure. But rather than cave in to it, Abbott takes a moment to compose himself on the pitching mound and actually whispers to himself, "Trust yourself, trust yourself."

This short statement of confidence is designed to keep himself under control and to let him "trust" his God-given athletic abilities. In doing this he regains his sense of purpose, his sense of play, and is then ready to go back to pitching.

This is a very simple way of psychologically "stepping back" from the competition for a few moments and catching one's breath. And this psychological breather is usually enough to let the athlete regain her perspective, return to the game, and let her practice-honed skills come shining through.

Try it with your little athletes. It works.

Take Care of Your Body and It'll Take Care of You

As mentioned, the best situation in sports is when the mind and body work together. But that isn't always possible, as injuries occur. Recently, there's been an increasing awareness of the kinds of physical injuries common to youth leagues. Scrapes, bumps, and bruises are to be expected and tolerated, but there are other more serious injuries that can be avoided.

While a discussion of the physical aspects of injury is not within the scope of this book, most parents know the terror of rushing to the aid of a child who has been hurt during the course of action. From a parenting point of view, it's important for your child to come to grips with injuries and to come away with a sense that physical hurts, in most cases, heal quite quickly.

In July of 1991, ABC News profiled the extent of physical injuries that occur in youth leagues. While the piece tried to be objective in its point of view, it was clear that each year several children suffer serious and some times fatal, injuries from playing in youth leagues.

The program pointed out that in 1990 alone, more than 140,000 kids from Dixie League, Little League, and Pony League baseball combined went to hospital emergency rooms. There was also the case of nine-year-old Ryan Wojick, killed during a Little League game when a pitched ball hit him in the chest, causing his heart to go into a fatal cardiac arrhythmia.

Certainly, this was a most rare accident. But the fact remains that over a ten-year period in the 1980s, 51 children were killed playing youth league baseball.

What does all this mean, besides scaring you? First off, you had better check out the playing equipment your kids use. For example, kids who play baseball and are under the age of ten should be using a soft, padded baseball, either the Flexiball, Kenko ball, or Worth's RIF (Reduced Injury Factor) ball. Regulation base balls are, in fact, as hard as rocks, and young kids are particularly vulnerable to getting hit in the face by a regular hardball. With the Flexiball, Kenko, or RIF ball, if they do get hit, the chances of serious injury are drastically reduced.

The same concerns apply to other potential contact sports, such as football, ice hockey, even soccer. Above all, make certain your child knows how to wear the equipment properly.

Second, too many coaches automatically assume that all kids know and understand how potentially dangerous each sport can be. Don't you make that assumption. Kids don't intuitively understand that by swinging a bat wildly they might accidentally clip another kid in the head. Kids who play ice hockey don't always understand why you're supposed to wear a helmet. Kids who play soccer don't automatically understand why you have to wear shin guards.

It's up to the coach—and to the parents—to explain to the kids why the protective equipment is there and how to use it.

Going back to the ABC News program, it was reported that Dr. Creighton Hale, the current president of Little League Baseball, has gone on the record as saying that he doesn't see "any serious issues pertaining to baseball/softball" safety. Yet in an article in the *Journal of Sports Medicine* published in 1979, Dr. Hale wrote: "Estimates are that there are 170,000 injuries to the face, eyes, and mouth each year. Some sort of facial protection could reduce injuries by 54,000."[1] Sure enough, many kids today wear face protectors on their batting helmets as extra protection against facial injuries.

Safety First ... Always
It should be obvious to all parents and coaches that safety should always be the top priority. Yet, this isn't always the case. Too many coaches either aren't aware of safety training with kids in sports, or they figure that the kids already know about safety practices.

Ironically, if there is one advantage organized youth leagues should have over spontaneous neighborhood pickup games, it is this: that coaches should teach from the first day all about safety on the field, whether it's being careful swinging a bat, learning how to slide properly, knowing how to strap on a helmet when playing ice hockey, or knowing when a child has had too much running around and needs something to drink.

But sad to say, too many parents still make the mistaken assumption that all coaches know all about children's safety. Again, while the scope of this book does not include sports injuries and ailments, the one point that ought to be taken from this section is that many kids' injuries are easily preventable if a responsible adult/parent spends a little time instructing and warning the kids properly about some of the hazards of playing organized sports.

Equal Opportunity

If you haven't noticed by now, this book has purposely treated young athletes ages five through 13, both boys and girls, pretty much the same when it comes to developing their athletic skills. There are several reasons for this. Consider that:

- Young boys and girls are physically similar in more ways than they are different.

- Boys and girls are equally aggressive and competitive when it comes to learning sports.

- Boys and girls are equally eager to win.

- For the most part, boys and girls readily accept the premise that they can play together on the same team and work toward the same team goals.

These premises, by the way, are not some hypothetical theories that I pulled out of the air, but are all based upon proven contemporary medical and psychological tests.[2]

Furthermore, since the adoption of Title IX in 1972, which amended the Civil Rights Act of 1964, girls and women have been afforded better access to the athletic education that boys and men have traditionally enjoyed over the years in the United States. That means that for over two decades now, boys and girls have been growing up, playing sports, and pursuing their dreams of athletic glory in high school and college.

What does all this mean to you as a coach or a parent? In sum, nothing more than that you should treat your boys and girls pretty much the same, making as little distinction as possible between the sexes. Yes, it's true that by the time they grow up and reach full physical maturity, the average male is five inches taller and thirty pounds heavier than the average female in this society. But we're talking about kids here, and if you have spent any time watching boys and girls in youth sports, you'll probably recognize that in many cases, it's the girls who dominate play at the earlier ages. Girls tend to mature faster physically than boys from ages five to eight, so it's not uncommon for girls to be the stars on coed teams.

As a Coach

If, as a coach, you find yourself running a coed team, the best approach is to keep everything unisex. For example, don't make any special exceptions for the girls, such as always having them play in positions far from the action or keeping them out of the game until the score is lopsided. Don't in any way make the girls feel as though they can't keep up with the boys, because, in fact, they can. Let the girls on your team get just as much quality playing time as your boys—and don't be surprised if the star or stars of your team are the ones with the ponytails.

As a Parent

Give your daughter the freedom to pursue any sport she wants to. Whether it's soccer, football, baseball, ice hockey, or gymnastics—whatever the sport—if she wants to try it, then by all means let her.

When she does go out for a sport, give her the same kind of encouragement, praise, and support that you would her brother. Victorious legal battles over the last 20 years have finally granted women in this country the right to pursue their athletic goals with the same freedom as men.

Keep in mind, for example, that back in the early 1970s Little League baseball fought a furious court battle to prevent girls from playing in their all-boy baseball league. That court battle was decided in favor of letting girls play, and today you'll find girls playing Little League baseball everywhere. In fact, as an extension of that coed involvement, the last few years has seen a woman first baseman play for an NCAA college baseball team on which all of her teammates were male. And last year a female placekicker kicked her first extra point in a real game while playing for a high school football team on Long Island, New York. Her teammates, all male, were thrilled for her.

The same line of reasoning regarding girls and boys in sports goes for the other youth leagues. Because of that court ruling on Little League, no league today can ban girls from playing in its organization. True, in some instances the girls don't want to compete with the boys. As a result, some soccer leagues, for example, split the boys and girls into two leagues, per the wishes of the kids and parents. But again, the phenomenon of boys and girls playing on the same team is now common in this country.

By the way, if your daughter happens to be placed on a team in which the coach doesn't see the kids as equal, then by all means make your concerns known. Coaches who espouse these so-called "traditionalist" views today are regarded as dinosaurs. By relegating your daughter to a secondary role on the team, such a coach is lowering her self-esteem and should be confronted about it.

You wouldn't like it if your child's teacher in school treated girls as second-class citizens with fewer academic abilities than the boys in her class. Equally, if you see a youth league coach treating your daughter in such a negative manner, don't wait an extra minute. Get on that coach's case right now.

What's the bottom line on boys and girls in youth sports? Simple. Treat them as equals. Sure, they're going to grow up and eventually find their own athletic preferences. But at this age you're only trying to get them to find out about team sports, to find out how much they enjoy playing them, and to make the experience fun.

The last time I checked, that's what every youth league charter says is the overall purpose for its participants. It shouldn't make any difference whether it's for boys or for girls.

1. Transcript from 20/20, ABC-TV, aired July 12, 1991.
2. S. Figler and G. Whitaker, *Sport & Play in American Life*, (Dubuque, Ia.: William C. Brown Publishers, 1991), p. 317.

CHAPTER 10

Alternative Approaches

Rob Nelson knows a lot about kids. He especially knows a lot about what kids like about sports.

There are those who say that Nelson, now 42, is still a kid himself. A kid who never had to grow up. And with that description Nelson would heartily agree.

Back in the mid-1970s, Nelson, a Cornell graduate, was playing minor league baseball in Portland, Oregon, when he and a teammate, former Yankee pitching great Jim Bouton, observed their teammates stuffing big wads of tobacco into their mouths and looking like, well, big leaguers. The way Nelson tells the story, both he and Bouton were disgusted with chewing tobacco. And they both recognized that tobacco chewing can cause cancer.

"The problem is," said Bouton to Nelson on that fateful evening, "kids like to emulate what big leaguers do. And for better or worse, big leaguers chew tobacco."

That's when Nelson struck upon an idea that reaped him and Bouton pure gold. Or in this case, pure gum.

"What if we took the same tinfoil pouch that chewing tobacco comes in," suggested Nelson, "and we replaced the tobacco with thin strips of bubble gum? In that way kids could get the feel that they're stuffing their mouths with tobacco, but in reality they would just be chewing gum. In fact, we could even call the bubble gum in a pouch something like 'Big League Chew.'"

And from that curious moment in a minor league bullpen, Big League Chew came into existence. The rest, as they say, is chewing-gum history.

Today, over 20 years later, Big League Chew pulls in millions of dollars each year in gross sales, as kids everywhere respond eagerly to Nelson's and Bouton's idea. The royalties that Nelson earns from the gum make him fairly wealthy, so he can spend his days literally going around the world playing baseball. So far he has played in such exotic spots as South Africa, Australia, Britain, Canada, and Holland.

But when he's not playing ball (he's a crafty left-handed pitcher), Nelson devotes a great deal of his time to working with youngsters. "If you want to know what kids are going to like," says the affable Nelson, "you've got to think like a kid. And that's exactly what I try to get across in my baseball camps."

Nelson's baseball camps are run every summer in various parts of the United States and are attended by boys and girls, ages six through twelve. "To me all that matters is that the kids learn to have fun. And having fun doesn't mean you necessarily have to be talented at playing the game."

Explains Nelson: "You see, too many coaches make the basic mistake that in order for a youngster to have fun playing baseball, he or she has to be an all-star. That's not only nonsense, it's also counterproductive. All that a kid wants to do is get better. See that they get better at mastering some of the skills they've worked on.

"I'll never forget what one mother told me—why she liked my baseball camp so much for her son. She said to me, 'He's been coming to your camp for four years now, and he still doesn't know he's not a very good player. All that matters to him is that he loves it."

To Nelson, that's what his camps are all about.

Thinking Like a Kid

As Nelson points out, it's probably been some time since you were a kid. So it might take a little effort to remember what kinds of things kids respond to.

"For example, any kid who follows baseball loves to hear the public address announcer at a baseball game. That's precisely why when each kid comes to bat in my camps, I make it a point that each player introduce himself and his favorite uniform number to all on hand. And if he has a favorite player on a favorite team, he or she can even combine that player's name with their own. So as a result, a kid will come to the plate and say very loudly, 'Now batting for the Braves, number 10, Matt Jones....'

"This works great because it allows the kid to live out the fantasy of being a big league star, and at the same time, it allows me, as the coach, to identify the child's face with his or her name.

"The point is, all kids, from age six up, have a favorite player. By making a big deal out of this public pronouncement, you're giving them a chance to feel good about themselves and, more importantly, to have fun doing it."

Having fun isn't the only priority in Nelson's camps. Learning the game is stressed as well. The difference is Nelson's camp tries to make the learning process much more enjoyable for the kids. "I use cartoon characters when I instruct them on the finer points of the game, " says Nelson. "For example, to get them to hold a bat properly, I introduce them to my favorite hitter of all time, Seymour Fingers."

It takes the kids a few moments to catch on to the pun of seeing more fingers when they grip the bat. "And that little cartoon character works like a charm in reminding kids how to hold the bat properly. All they have to do is remember Seymour Fingers."

Nelson uses all sorts of characters when teaching baseball. His fertile imagination has introduced his campers to Vicious Hits (who always forms a V shape with his front arm when he swings the bat), Tiny Steps (who's known for his very small stride when hitting), Tiny's twin brother, Pointer Steps, and so on.

"The beauty of why this works," explains Nelson, a former elementary school teacher, "is that kids have a much easier time remembering correct procedures if they equate those instructions with funny phrases or characters."

When teaching kids how to throw a ball properly, Nelson reminds them that when they are about to throw the ball, they should always remember to make an L with their throwing arm (keep their elbow bent a bit). "By making that L, they're always reminded that they 'love' to throw a ball."

Other Fun Teaching Devices

Nelson uses all sorts of improvised and spontaneous ploys to keep his kids enthused and happy. "One of the most popular gimmicks is the 'instant replay' rule I have. That is, if a kid is fielding and he or she makes a terrific play, then I'll stop all the action on the diamond and I'll call for an instant replay. The star of the moment then has to replay, in slow motion, the great fielding play that he or she has just made. Again, it's a great positive reinforcer for the kids and they all get a big kick out of being asked to do an instant replay."

Nelson also occasionally attempts to instruct the kids on the nature of baseball; that is, that the game of baseball involves a great deal of frustration ." Let's face it, in baseball you can hit a ball right on the nose—a line drive shot—only to see it caught by an opposing player. It's a game where, if you're going to play, you have to come to grips with frustration."

To help teach the kids this lesson, Nelson will often position himself as the sole umpire of the game. "Let's say a batter hits a ball that is definitely foul by about two or three feet. All the kids see that it's a foul ball. But as the umpire, I might call it a fair ball.

"The kids in the field start to scream and holler about such a lousy call. But it's precisely at those moments, I tell them that in baseball, as in life, many times things just aren't fair. And either you can sulk and get mad or play by the decision that was made by the umpire. Before too long I find that the kids begin to accept my calls, both foul and fair, as being just part of the game, and they continue to play hard."

Nelson also subscribes to the practice of teaching kids by reinforcing good, specific behavior. "I never use the word 'but' with any youngster. I never say to a player, 'Hey, you looked good out there today, but . . .' I just don't do that. Kids know instinctively when you use the word but that something negative is coming. So as a matter of course, I praise them and compliment them on what they're doing well, and I leave it at that."

Nelson is also aware that kids like to keep score when they play games. "The ones who know how to count and keep score invariably do. But when anybody asks me the score during the course of a game, I take my time, think for a few seconds, and invariably, the score is always tied. I don't get into a discussion about it; I tell the kids just to keep playing. And you know what? After a while they stop asking me what the score is. They just keep on having fun."

There's that key word again. Fun. Just how important is having fun to kids? According to a major poll of more than 10,000 kids nationwide, conducted recently by the Youth Sports Institute of Michigan State University, fun is still the top priority. In this particular study the kids were given a choice of twelve reasons to play sports. Of the twelve, fun was the top choice for both boys and girls. Winning was ranked eighth for boys and dead last for the girls. [1]

Setting Up an Alternative League

If there's one overriding point that Rob Nelson makes with his unusual approach to teaching baseball, it's that as a parent you don't have to assume that the traditional organized youth leagues are the only game in town. Sure, if Little League or AYSO or U.S.A. ice hockey is already a long-standing tradition in your community, fine. Unless, of course, you don't think your child is finding enough satisfaction or enjoyment from those leagues or you have a problem with the way the leagues are being run or a concern about the coaching.

As an alternative you might try starting your own independent youth team. No, you don't need to get sponsors, uniforms, umpires, or really anything else. All you need is a place to play, lots of enthusiasm, and if you're lucky, perhaps the blessing of the town's recreation department.

Example: In the town where I live, soccer is very popular with kids, mainly because it is a relatively easy game for kids to learn and because all you really need to play is a soccer ball, some shin guards, and two teams.

Because of the weather soccer is played only in the spring and the fall in Armonk, New York. Yet, a few years ago one of the dads in town, Rob Morris, decided it would be great if kids could keep on playing during the cold winter months when snow covers the fields.

His solution? Morris called the elementary school to see if the gym was being used on Saturday mornings. It turned out that the gym was empty, and Morris quickly made a few calls to gain the permission of the school to use it for an hour on Saturdays. Within a few weeks Morris had more than 24 kids playing indoor soccer. No uniforms, no official team standings, no parents. Just a bunch of kids split up into two teams, playing soccer, and making up fair rules as situations arose.

Morris, a former elementary school teacher and now an insurance executive, looked upon his innovation as nothing more than "a little enthusiasm combined with a little common sense. After all, nobody was using the gym, the kids love to play soccer, and combining the two seemed only natural."

Example: When I started my baseball clinic in Armonk, it wasn't because I felt that Little League baseball in our town was necessarily wrong or poorly done. Rather, it was my experience after watching a number of Little League games that it seemed that many of the kids just weren't having much fun. It seemed as though they played simply because Mom and Dad wanted them to, and let's face it, baseball can be a real drag if there isn't much action.

So, I devised my own baseball clinic in conjunction with the town rec department. I got access to a town field, and we have practice every weekend for an hour and a half. During that time I try to take a few tips from Rob Nelson's bag of tricks, and I also try to keep the kids busy all the time. I teach them how to hold and throw a ball, how to round the bases, how to chew bubble gum, how to crack open sunflower seeds, and how to make chatter like a real major leaguer.

In between we take batting practice, do rundown drills, field plays, and so forth. The point is, by the time the session comes to an end, the kids are exhausted but full of fun and satisfaction. They've been busy playing ball.

To help me out I ask a few fathers and mothers to assist. Again, all strictly voluntary. No parades. No official standings. No umpires. But the kids learn and master their baseball skills by playing. Playing with no pressure on them.

These are just two small examples. There are all sorts of possibilities. All that's needed is a little parental enthusiasm, some basic equipment, and a desire to have fun.

Playing Sports with Your Child
Of all sporting activities, remember that there are very few moments more gratifying than those in which a parent actively plays with his or her son or daughter. One of the vital lessons that too many parents forget is that they can join in the fun and games of their kids. The only requirement is that they must put themselves in the role of kids again.

Children love nothing more than having a mom or dad get involved in a spontaneous game of soccer, volleyball, running bases, tag—just about any sporting event. Not only does the moment carry with it a sense of pure enjoyment for both parent and child, but it also establishes a rare channel of communication in which they can relate to each other on the same level.

The trick as mentioned is for parents to play at their children's level:

- If there's a dispute on a call, let the majority among the kids rule. Don't let yourself be pegged as the adult arbiter. Why? Because you'll soon end up in the role of umpire or referee and that will place you on a level above your children. Rather than bringing them closer to you, you'll be putting up barriers.

- Let the kids make up the teams. Don't allow yourself to participate on the adult level. Rather, you play with a skill commensurate to your child's age. That makes for a fair competition. If your child is ten, then you play like a ten-year-old. If your child is eight, then you play with the skill of an eight-year-old, and so on.

- Be flexible. Go along with what the kids want, not what you want. Let them lead you, rather than the other way around. Be a follower, rather than the instructor. You'll be surprised at just how creative and resourceful your children can be.

- Be careful not to impose "adult" ideas. That is, let the kids decide what the rules, boundaries, and teams are going to be. Even if some of their ideas aren't very sound (from an adult's perspective, that is), let them work it out. After all, if kids don't get any experience in working out their problems together, they'll really run into difficulties when they get older.

- Don't coach the kids. This is not the time to do any coaching with tips on how your child or her friends could play the game better. Kids have minds of their own, and they usually resent when a grown-up comes in and tries to tell them how they could do something better. Keep in mind that they think they already know more about the game they're playing than you do. If you start offering free advice, you're going to ruin the game and alienate the kids.

Be Creative

One of the best ways to let you and your children enjoy each other's company is to develop your own special family game. It makes no difference where you live, because these kinds of games can take place indoors or outdoors, summer or winter. For example, when I was growing up, we invented a very simple game in our household that we still play today and have actually passed on to the next generation.

All this game needs is some balled-up socks and a small empty trash can, the kind you would find in an office. Then, we place the trash can about ten or 15 feet away, and we all take turns trying to throw a balled-up sock into the can from behind a line. Sort of like miniature free-throw shooting. We allow each participant ten shots at a time, and we play several rounds. The player with the best score at the end wins.

Perhaps as simple a game as you could design. But it's easy enough for all kids to understand, and it's easy enough for all to play. Remember kids like games that are simple to learn and easy to do.

When it comes to inventing games, kids have amazing creative abilities. They can make an enjoyable game out of throwing a tennis ball against a wall. Or even combine games like baseball and soccer into their own new sport. The point is, it's up to the parent to encourage the child to explore new athletic possibilities. And be careful not to inject too much parental instruction into their own brand of fun.

What about the Future?

If there's one truth about kids and sports, it's that they will always seek out those activities that bring them the most fun and the most self-satisfaction. Psychologists often point out that all people tend to do what is perceived to be in their best interests. With kids—whether it's the 1990s, the 1970s, or the 2010s—the simple fact of the matter is, they will always pursue those activities in life that bring them the most pleasure.

Coupling enjoyment with rising self-esteem is precisely where sports help children. When they're just learning the games, you play a vital role in terms of encouragement, praise, and a bit of instruction. As the child grows into organized youth leagues, it can be emotionally trying as a parent to see how your little loved one matches up against the other kids his age. But that, of course, is part of the growing-up process—not only for the child, but also for you, the parent.

One of the themes of this book has been to show that organized youth leagues are not necessarily unhealthy for your child; rather, they can be the source of wonderful, healthy, happy experiences, so long as the parents/ adults who run the league keep their priorities in order. I have also stressed that you, as an adult and parent, must be just as involved in your child's athletic development as you are in his academic development.

As you watch your child continue to grow and develop into junior high school and high school sports, there will be a shift in priorities. At those levels the coaches (most of whom are professional educators employed by your school) are going to stress winning as the number-one goal of the teams. Again, that is not necessarily a bad development, because by that age your children want to see positive results from their hard efforts at practice. Winning is a fine goal and should be striven for, as long as the coaches keep a reasonable perspective.

You should continue to stay involved in your child's development as an athlete. Yes, there are those parents who become too involved, overbearing. That's why it's important for you to keep the emotions on an even keel, to allow your child to enjoy her moment in the sun of youth sports. There's nothing wrong with fully embracing and enjoying your son or daughter's athletic achievements—so long as you fully recognize and realize that it is your son or daughter who is achieving out on the athletic fields and not you.

If you want your children to enjoy sports for a lifetime, always bear in mind that a large portion of the satisfaction they receive from sports comes from the way in which you dole out your parental love, support, and encouragement. If your child is lucky enough to have developed some athletic skills, then let her know it with your support.

I'll leave off with this one note. Last year on a cloudy, rainy day in which showers soaked the field, I was called on to be the referee in an organized youth league soccer game. Just before the game got started, a mother of one of the players grabbed me by the arm and said quite seriously, "You're not going to let them play, are you?"

When I replied that a few raindrops wouldn't hurt, she scolded me, adding that she didn't want her child catching pneumonia because of my unprofessional attitude. After I tried to reassure the mother that her child wouldn't melt and that kids actually like to play in the rain, she stomped off, convinced I was a lunatic.

The game started. The kids on both sides were six- or seven-years-old, and despite the sloppy field and the pouring rain, the action was furious at both ends of the field.

About midway in the third quarter, one team was controlling the ball as best as it could, and one youngster ran up to the ball and kicked it with all his might. As he did so, he slipped in the mud and fell on his fanny. The ball, meanwhile, rolled about ten yards, where a player from an opposing team tried to kick the ball back in the opposite direction. But as she tried to muster a hefty shot, she, too, slipped in the mud.

Upon seeing this wet and wild exchange, all the kids on both teams opened up and laughed heartily for several moments. It was that kind of pure spontaneous laughter that you cherish in your children—the kind you'd like to bottle and keep for posterity.

But the point was made. I turned to one of the fathers who was coaching and asked, "Say, when was the last time you actually heard kids like these actually laugh out loud during a youth league game?"

Needless to say, the dad was hard pressed to answer the question.

Perhaps, it was the rain-soaked field. Perhaps, it was the fact that both kids had slipped while trying to chase and kick the ball. Perhaps, it was the moment of just playing the game.

But best of all—perhaps, they were just having fun.

1. *The Philadelphia Inquirer*, August 30, 1991.

SOURCES

In Addition To Those
Listed As Chapter Endnotes

American Youth Soccer Organization (AYSO) Under-8 Coaching Manual, published by AYSO's National Coaching Commission, Los Angeles, Ca. 1990.

Children and Youth in Competitive Sports, by Bryant Cratty. Baldwin, N.Y.: Educational Activities, Inc., 1974.

"Children Say Having Fun Is Number One," *USA Today,* September 10, 1990.

"Children's Sports: Fun Outranks Winning," *The Philadelphia Inquirer,* August 30, 1991.

Coaching Young Athletes, Rainer Martens, Ph.D., ed. Champaign, Ill.: Human Kinetics Publishers, 1981.

Dear Dr. Psych: A Kids' Guide to Handling Sports Problems, by Nate Zinsser, Ph.D. New York: Time-Warner, Inc., 1991.

"Fathers and Their Athletic Children: A Fragile Partnership," *Rockland Journal-News* (White Plains, N.Y.), June 16, 1991.

"Fields of Dreams: Little League's Not So Little Anymore," *Sport,* September 1989.

"Helping to Develop Confidence in Sports Activities," *The New York Times,* July 4, 1991.

"Hockey Doctor's Unique Rx," *Sport,* July 1991.

"Homegrown Fury Drives Dibble's Pitching Life," *The Hartford Courant,* June 23, 1991.

"How to Foster Self-esteem," *The New York Times Magazine,* April 28, 1991.

"Is Your Child Ready for Team Sports?" *Parents,* May 1991.

"It's a Kids' Game," *The Hartford Courant,* April 10, 1991.

Joy and Sadness in Children's Sports, by Rainer Martens, Ph.D. Champaign, Ill.: Human Kinetics Publishers, 1978.

"Kids in Sports: Pushed Too Hard?" *Scholastic News,* March 15, 1991.

"Kill the Ump? Apparently, Coach Tried," *The New York Daily News,* June 23, 1991.

"Law to Protect Baseball Umpires," *ABCA Newsletter,* Au gust 1991.

Leadership Training for Little League Managers and Coaches, by Tom Kerley, M.A., published by Little League Baseball, Inc. Williamsport, Pa. 1991.

Little League: Today's Youth, Tomorrow's Leaders, published by Little League Baseball, Inc. Williamsport, Pa. 1991.

"A Little League Coach Shares His Secrets," *The New York Times,* August 24, 1991.

Little League Confidential, by Bill Geist. New York: Macmillan, 1992.

The Little League Game: How Kids, Coaches, and Parents Really Play It, by Lewis Yablonsky. New York: Times Books, 1979.

"The Other Side: A Manager's Guide to Working with Little Leaguers," published by Little League Baseball, Inc. Williamsport, Pa. 1991.

"Playing Hardball," transcript from ABC News show *20/20* aired July 12, 1991.

Pony League Baseball and Softball Blue Book, published by Pony Baseball, Inc. Washington, Pa. 1990.

"Psychologists Take Seat on Little League Bench," *The New York Times,* March 14, 1988.

"Safer at the Plate," *Detroit Free Press,* April 2, 1991.

Sport & Play in American Life, by Stephen K. Figler and Gail Whitaker. Dubuque, Ia.: William C. Brown Publishers, 1991.

"Stress-Free Little League," *Sports Illustrated,* August 22, 1988.

"Touch All the Bases," *USA Today,* April 18, 1991.

"Whose Game Is It, Anyway?" Ruth Pennebaker, *Parents,* October 1991, p. 90.

"Why Don't the Kids Seem to Be Having Fun in Little League? The Deterrent Is the Adults," essay by Jay Feldman in *Newsweek,* May 22, 1989.

"Why Young People Play . .. Or Quit," *Scholastic Coach,* September 1991.

"Working Out a Strategy to Shape Up Flabby Kids," *USA Today,* August 7, 1991.

"World Series Dynasty: Why Taiwan Reigns," *Sport,* September 1989.

About the Author

Rick Wolff

Rick Wolff is a nationally recognized expert in the field of athletic performance enhancement. A former professional baseball player and successful college coach, Wolff served as the roving psychological coach for the Cleveland Indians from 1989 to 1994. Over the years, he has worked with top athletes from Major League Baseball, the National Football League, the National Hockey League, tennis players, golfers, and more. An honors graduate of Harvard and Long Island University, Wolff is the author of numerous books and articles on sports psychology. He lives in Armonk, New York, with his wife and three children.

ADDITIONAL RESOURCES FROM SPORTS PUBLISHING INC

A VIDEO COMPANION TO GOOD SPORTS©!

I recently completed a video companion to this book entitled "KIDS SPORTS, A Family Guide©." The video features San Francisco 49er MVP quarterback Steve Young and is produced by Michael Bloom and DHB & Associates, Inc. The video is a perfect illustration of many of the topics discussed in this book. Family viewing of "KIDS SPORTS, A Family Guide©" allows you and your children to learn to balance safety, competition and fun together! I am certain it will open new avenues of communication between parents, coaches and children. I recommend it wholeheartedly.

In making the video, I spent several hours with Steve Young, and his comments and viewpoints on the importance of understanding youth sports are refreshing and genuine. The video is worth its purchase price just to hear Steve's heartfelt comments and insights.

To acquire the video, you can go to your local video store and purchase it for $19.95, or you can order it directly from DHB & Associates Inc. Either way, I feel you should complement this book by acquiring "KIDS SPORTS, A Family Guide©."

Rick Wolff